Wisdom Keepers

Registered Charity SC038225
Registered Company SC322915

21a Grosvenor Crescent
EDINBURGH EH12 5EL
Tel: 0131 346 7981

Email: info@fiop.org.uk
Website: fiop@dioceseofedinburgh.org

Wisdom Keepers

A Resource for Faith Sharing Among Seniors

Wisdom keepers
are those who
have the resources
to share what they
have learned from
life's experience
and pass it on to
future generations.

Sharan A. Benton

Saint Mary's Press
Christian Brothers Publications
Winona, Minnesota

Genuine recycled paper with 10% post-consumer waste.
Printed with soy-based ink.

The publishing team included Carl Koch, development editor; Cheryl Drivdahl, copy editor; Brooke E. Saron, production editor; Hollace Storkel, typesetter; Cären Yang, cover designer; pre-press, printing, and binding by the graphics division of Saint Mary's Press.

Cover photo: PhotoDisc, Inc., 1999

Printed in the United States of America

Printing: 9 8 7 6 5 4 3 2 1

Year: 2008 07 06 05 04 03 02 01 00

ISBN 0-88489-626-9

Contents

Preface

Prayer and faith-sharing groups, Bible study groups, and other gatherings of seniors have formed in many congregations. Older members of the church face different challenges to their faith than do younger people. They are reflecting on new issues, problems, and opportunities.

The Office of Ministry and Spirituality of the Archdiocese of Louisville created this book because those ministering to groups of seniors found that resources specifically designed to help older congregants simply did not exist. The people who used *Wisdom Keepers: A Resource for Faith Sharing Among Seniors* within the diocese responded with enthusiasm.

The book offers reflections on forty-six themes. Each reflection contains an introduction, a Scripture passage, reflection questions, petitions, and a concluding prayer. Though the reflections were primarily intended for use by groups, individuals have found them helpful too.

Using the Reflections in Groups

Congregations in the Louisville archdiocese have adopted *Wisdom Keepers* as the focus of monthly meetings, retreats, or days of reflection.

In parishes in which senior groups already exist, each monthly or bimonthly gathering begins with a reflection from *Wisdom Keepers*. After praying and reflecting, the participants eat a lunch or potluck supper together.

Some organizing groups select the topics for a series of gatherings, publish a brochure listing the title for each session, and distribute the brochure throughout the senior community. Some choose topics from meeting to meeting.

Because the format of the reflections is simple and direct, the meetings are easy to conduct. A leader or leaders may read the theme. Someone else may read the Scripture passage. Some silence for prayer and reflection might follow. Discussion of the questions on the Scripture passage and the personal questions typically consumes most of the gathering time. Offering the petitions gives the participants time to pray. The concluding prayer may be proclaimed by one person or recited by the entire group.

The reflections are easily adaptable. For instance, depending on the group's schedule, the questions on the Scripture passage might be skipped, or they might be discussed as part of the petitions.

Using the Reflections As an Individual

Josephine Miklic, SL, of the pastoral care department at the Loretto Infirmary, uses single reflections with individuals who are confronting particular situations. For instance, she shared the reflection "The Loss of a Child" with a nurse at the infirmary who had just lost one of her children.

Other individuals have simply used reflections as issues arose in their life. Sister Josephine has found the reflection "Resurrection" to help people close to death. She has used the reflection "Giving Up Activities We Always Enjoyed" with many individuals who struggled with letting go.

If you keep a journal or diary, you may find the reflections to be good starting points for your writing. Or you may wish to simply sit silently and pray over the reflections.

God is always abiding with us as we pray. So be assured that no matter how you use the reflections, God will be with you, calling you to wisdom and to sharing.

Thanks

Wisdom Keepers has been developed as a collaborative effort. The following people need to be thanked: Sharon Bailey, Liz Bindner, Mary Byrne, Mary Cheap, Sal Della Bella, Suzanne Hasson, Michelle Herberger, Miriam Hixenbaugh, Marti Jewell, Jim Keegan, SJ, Rosemary McAdam, Rev. Bob Stuempel, and Judy Thomas.

May all who share these reflections find peace, joy, hope, and deeper faith. May you embrace the wisdom of your years and share it with everyone.

The Wisdom of Elders

We are a generation of "wisdom keepers" who have much wisdom and life experience to hand on to younger generations. We have a responsibility to share what we have learned from life with our children, with our family, and with our friends. God has gifted us with the wisdom of age to pass on to those who will listen. We need to be persistent because seniors are sometimes not listened to, simply because of their age.

Reading: Help to Speak Wisdom (Wisdom 7:15–28)

May God grant me to speak with judgment,
and to have thoughts worthy of what I have received;
for he is the guide even of wisdom
and the corrector of the wise.
For both we and our words are in his hand,
as are all understanding and skill in crafts.

. . . .

I learned both what is secret and what is manifest,
for wisdom, the fashioner of all things, taught me.

There is in her a spirit that is intelligent, holy,
unique, manifold, subtle,
mobile, clear, unpolluted,
distinct, invulnerable, loving the good, keen,
irresistible, beneficent, humane,
steadfast, sure, free from anxiety,

all-powerful, overseeing all,
and penetrating through all spirits
that are intelligent, pure, and altogether subtle.
For wisdom is more mobile than any motion;
because of her pureness she pervades and penetrates
all things.
For she is a breath of the power of God,
and a pure emanation of the glory of the Almighty;
therefore nothing defiled gains entrance into her.
For she is a reflection of eternal light,
a spotless mirror of the working of God,
and an image of his goodness.
Although she is but one, she can do all things,
and while remaining in herself, she renews all things;
in every generation she passes into holy souls
and makes them friends of God, and prophets;
for God loves nothing so much as the person who lives
with wisdom.

Questions on the Scripture Passage

- How does wisdom teach us about the friendship of God?
- What is the nature of wisdom?
- How is wisdom the image of God's goodness?
- Is there a difference between wisdom and knowledge? Explain.

Personal Questions

- What are some wise things you have learned over the years? What does society need to hear from you?
- What is one story or event you want to pass on to the next generation?
- Who was a wisdom keeper in your life?

Petitions

For those who share their life experience with others, we pray . . .

In gratitude for the years of life we have had and the wisdom we have gained, we pray . . .

(Add your own intentions.)

Concluding Prayer

Holy Wisdom, you have given us the wisdom to know that our life depends on you alone. Help us to share our wisdom with those around us, and to gain our strength from good friends and the best friend of all, Jesus the Christ. Amen.

Additional resource. *From Age-ing to Sage-ing: A Profound New Vision of Growing Older,* by Zalman Schachter-Shalomi and Ronald S. Miller (Warner Books).

Jesus Rose and the Spirit Came

Jesus' mission on this earth can only be completed with the coming of the Spirit and our choice to continue the work of the church. In our life, in our church, and in the world, we have seen moments when the Spirit is at work. One example is when the Second Vatican Council called us to full, conscious, and active participation in the liturgical life of the church. Another example is when our faith alone helps us through a crisis in our life. Another is when we reach out to the world.

Reading: The Coming of the Paraclete (John 16:5–33)

Now I am going to him who sent me. . . . I tell you the truth: it is to your advantage that I go away, for if I do not go away, the Advocate will not come to you; but if I go, I will send him to you. . . .

. . . When the Spirit of truth comes, he will guide you into all the truth; for he will not speak on his own, but will speak whatever he hears, and he will declare to you the things that are to come. He will glorify me, because he will take what is mine and declare it to you. . . .

. . . Very truly, I tell you, you will weep and mourn, but . . . your pain will turn into joy. When a woman is in labor, she has pain, because her hour has come. But when her child is born, she no longer remembers the anguish because of the joy of having brought a human being into the world. So you have pain now; but I will see you again, and your hearts will rejoice, and no one will take your joy from you. . . .

. . . The Father himself loves you, because you have loved me and have believed that I came from God.

Questions on the Scripture Passage

- Why, do you think, does Jesus say, "It is to your advantage that I go away"?
- In this Scripture passage, how does Jesus ask the disciples for their trust in waiting for the Spirit to come?
- In this passage, what is Jesus saying about God's love for us?

Personal Questions

- Do you believe that the Spirit works in our lives? How have you experienced the Spirit?
- As followers of Jesus, do we have a responsibility to bring the message of Jesus into our homes, neighborhoods, and workplaces? If so, how are we to do that?
- Do you think the Spirit was working at the Second Vatican Council and has been working in the church since the council ended? If so, how?

Petitions

That the spirit of God will continue to work in our lives and our congregation, we pray . . .

That our understanding of the Trinity will deepen our faith life, we pray . . .

(Add your own intentions.)

Concluding Prayer

Christ Jesus, we know you left this earth so that the spirit of God can live among us. Help us to be aware of the Spirit working in us and in our world. We place our trust in you who rose so that the Spirit could come. Amen.

Additional resource. *A Spirituality of Relationships,* by Don Kimball (Don Bosco Multimedia).

Jesus' Command to Love

John's Gospel gives us insight into how we are called to love as Jesus loved and to abide in his love. This command to love ultimately leads us to live more freely. By loving as Jesus, we bear witness to the unconditional love of God in our world.

Reading: A Disciple's Love (John 15:9–17)

As the Father has loved me, so I have loved you; abide in my love. If you keep my commandments, you will abide in my love, just as I have kept my Father's commandments and abide in his love. I have said these things to you so that my joy may be in you, and that your joy may be complete.

This is my commandment, that you love one another as I have loved you. No one has greater love than this, to lay down one's life for one's friends. You are my friends if you do what I command you. I do not call you servants any longer, because the servant does not know what the master is doing; but I have called you friends, because I have made known to you everything that I have heard from my Father. You did not choose me but I chose you. And I appointed you to go and bear fruit, fruit that will last, so that the Father will give you whatever you ask him in my name. I am giving you these commands so that you may love one another.

Questions on the Scripture Passage

- According to the Scripture passage, when do we receive the gift of joy?
- What does the Gospel of John say about how we are to love our friends?
- According to Jesus, what is the command to love?
- How are we friends of Jesus?

Personal Questions

- What are some stories of how you live the commandment of love?
- Not counting Jesus, have any persons "laid down their lives" for you?
- Who has loved you?

Petitions

For those who have died for others, especially in war or accidents, we pray . . .

For the times we have reached out in love and been rejected, we pray . . .

(Add your own intentions.)

Concluding Prayer

Jesus, you give us the command to love as you loved. What a challenge to bring that love to all we meet. Be with us as we walk our journey of faith, and teach us to love by your example. Amen.

Additional resource. *Children's Letters to God,* compiled by Stuart Hample (Workman Publishing Co.).

Church Picnics, Socials, and Fish Fries

In parish life, organizing a picnic, social, or fish fry can be hard and exhausting, but rewarding. Many people come together with different gifts to make the event successful. The experience is wonderful because of the way the community works to get the job done. Seeds sown in this effort help build a spirit of community that enables all members to celebrate when they gather for prayer and liturgy at Mass.

Reading: The Parable of the Seed (Matthew 13:4–23)

[Jesus said,] "As he sowed, some seeds fell on the path, and the birds came and ate them up. Other seeds fell on rocky ground, where they did not have much soil, and they sprang up quickly, since they had no depth of soil. But when the sun rose, they were scorched; and since they had no root, they withered away. Other seeds fell among thorns, and the thorns grew up and choked them. Other seeds fell on good soil and brought forth grain, some a hundredfold, some sixty, some thirty. Let anyone with ears listen!"

Then the disciples came and asked him, "Why do you speak to them in parables?" He answered, . . . "The reason I speak to them in parables is that 'seeing they do not perceive, and hearing they do not listen, nor do they understand.' . . .

"Hear then the parable of the sower. When anyone hears the word of the kingdom and does not understand it, the evil one comes and snatches away what is sown in the heart; this is what was sown on the path. As for what was sown on rocky ground, this is the one who hears the word and immediately receives it with joy; yet such a person has no root, but endures only for a while, and when trouble or persecution arises on account of the word, that person immediately falls away. As for what was sown among thorns, this is the one who hears the word, but the cares of the world and the lure of wealth choke the word, and it yields nothing. But as for what was sown on good soil, this is the one who hears the word and understands it, who indeed bears fruit and yields, in one case a hundredfold, in another sixty, and in another thirty."

Questions on the Scripture Passage

- Why, do you think, does Jesus speak in parables?
- Why, do you think, does Jesus talk about listening and seeing as important?
- When you think of the Reign of God, what images come to mind?

Personal Questions

- How do you practice your faith and put it into action?
- What story can you share about a church picnic or social or fish fry?
- What happens when a church community works and celebrates together?

Petitions

For the people who work hard to make parish events and socials rewarding, we pray . . .

For those who spread the Word of God through teaching and preaching, we pray . . .

(Add your own intentions.)

Concluding Prayer

God, you gave us the Scriptures and parables to teach us about living. We have examples of how to be fully human. Guide us to be loving, caring people who plant and sow seeds by the works we do. We make this prayer through Jesus, who is our example of working and celebrating. Amen.

Additional resource. *Stories of Coming Home: Finding Spirituality in Our Messy Lives,* by William John Fitzgerald (Paulist Press).

Births and Hope

Imagine the experience of hope while we wait for a child to be born: the excitement of other children in the family, the expectation of a child or grandchild. Emotions of all kinds are a part of this birth journey. What hopes and dreams do we have for this child? Times such as this make us excited, give us life, and offer us hope for the future of family. They are wonderful moments for reflecting on our children's births and all that they will bring to our families for years to come.

Reading: Hannah Bears a Son (1 Samuel 1:19–27)

They rose early in the morning and worshiped before the Lord; then they went back to their house at Ramah. Elkanah knew his wife Hannah, and the Lord remembered her. In due time Hannah conceived and bore a son. She named him Samuel, for she said, "I have asked him of the Lord."

The man Elkanah and all his household went up to offer to the Lord the yearly sacrifice, and to pay his vow. But Hannah did not go up, for she said to her husband, "As soon as the child is weaned, I will bring him, that he may appear in the presence of the Lord, and remain there forever; I will offer him as a nazirite for all time." Her husband Elkanah said to her, "Do what seems best to you, wait until you have weaned him; only—may the Lord establish his word." So the woman remained and nursed her son, until she weaned him. When she had weaned him, she took him up with her, along with a three-year-old bull, an ephah of flour, and a skin of wine. She brought him to the house of the LORD at Shiloh; and the child was young. Then they slaughtered the bull, and they brought the child to Eli. And she said, "Oh, my lord! As you live, my lord, I am the woman who was standing here in your presence, praying to the LORD. For this child I prayed; and the LORD has granted me the petition that I made to him."

Questions on the Scripture Passage

- What is Hannah's prayer to God?
- Why is it so important for Hannah to go to the temple and offer thanks to God?
- Is her husband, Elkanah, pleased to have a son? Why or why not?

Personal Questions

- What is it like to want a child and not conceive, or to want a child and get pregnant or adopt?
- Families used to be much larger. What were the advantages and challenges of larger families?
- What are your hopes and dreams for children in today's world?

Petitions

That parents and grandparents will take time to enjoy their children, we pray . . .

That we will give our children roots for stability and wings for flight, we pray . . .

(Add your own intentions.)

Concluding Prayer

God, help us to be grateful for the gift of new life in the birth of a child. Bless family life and the raising of children; give parents wisdom and courage in guiding their children. Amen.

Additional resource. *Birth and Baptism,* by Saint Mary's Press, TalkPoints for Families series (Saint Mary's Press).

The Gift of Grandchildren

What wonderful gifts grandchildren are! They keep us active, they teach us patience, they help us take time to play, and they keep our hearts young. They help us remember that life is wonderful and exciting, as it reveals itself to them and us.

Reading: Jesus Blesses the Children (Mark 10:13–16)

People were bringing little children to him in order that he might touch them; and the disciples spoke sternly to them. But when Jesus saw this, he was indignant and said to them, "Let the little children come to me; do not stop them; for it is to such as these that the kingdom of God belongs. Truly I tell you, whoever does not receive the kingdom of God as a little child will never enter it." And he took them up in his arms, laid his hands on them, and blessed them.

Questions on the Scripture Passage

- Why, do you think, are people bringing their children to Jesus?
- What does Jesus say the children will inherit? What do you think that means?
- How are children treated in Jesus' day?
- Why, do you think, is it important for Jesus to embrace, bless, and hug the children?

Personal Questions

- What happens to your spirit when you are with children, especially your grandchildren?
- Why are we to be childlike?
- How does it feel to embrace, hug, and bless children, especially your grandchildren?

Petitions

That all children will experience the appropriate and loving embrace of an adult, we pray . . .

For all sick and dying children, that someone will give them unconditional love, we pray . . .

(Add your own intentions.)

Concluding Prayer

Loving God, help us to be an example of your unconditional love, to all children, especially our grandchildren. Help us to share our gift of time with them. We ask this in the name of Jesus, who embraced, hugged, and blessed all children. Amen.

Additional resources. *Love You Forever*, by Robert Munsch (Firefly Books).

Those caring for grandchildren may like the free book *Resource Guide for Grandparents,* available through the Jefferson County Attorney's Office, Legal Arts Building, Suite 501, 200 South Seventh Street, Louisville, KY 40202; phone 502-574-5500.

Prayer for Those Who Are Sick

Often we are asked to pray for someone who is sick, or we ask for prayers when we are ill. Praying for those who are sick is a wonderful gift. We continue to build up the Body of Christ as we remember one another in prayer. As a community we pray for one another at Mass, especially when we say the Our Father.

READING: THE OUR FATHER
(MATTHEW 6:8–15; SEE ALSO LUKE 11:1–4)

Do not be like them, for your Father knows what you need before you ask him.

Pray then in this way:

Our Father in heaven,
hallowed be your name.
Your kingdom come.
Your will be done,
on earth as it is in heaven.
Give us this day our daily bread.
And forgive us our debts,
as we also have forgiven our debtors.
And do not bring us to the time of trial,
but rescue us from the evil one.

For if you forgive others their trespasses, your heavenly Father will also forgive you; but if you do not forgive others, neither will your Father forgive your trespasses.

Questions on the Scripture Passage

- Why do we say the Our Father together during worship in our church?
- When someone is sick or dying and hears the Our Father, how do they respond to it?
- Why, do you think, did Jesus leave this prayer for us to say?

Personal Questions

- How do you think saying the Our Father helps us to pray for one another?
- Do you pray for others? Do you ask others to pray for you?
- Have you experienced the healing power of prayer?

Petitions

For all those who have asked us to pray for them, we pray . . .

For all our friends who are ill, we pray . . .

(Add your own intentions.)

Concluding Prayer

Our Father who art in heaven,
hallowed be thy name.
Thy Kingdom come.
Thy will be done on earth, as it is in heaven.

Give us this day our daily bread,
and forgive us our trespasses,
  as we forgive those who trespass against us,
and lead us not into temptation,
but deliver us from evil.
Amen.

ADDITIONAL RESOURCE. *WomanWisdom: A Feminist Lectionary and Psalter,* by Miriam Therese Winter (Crossroad Publishing Co.).

Interdependence

As we grow older, we realize that we cannot do the things we did in our youth, at least not as fast. We have slowed down, which is not a bad thing. In some ways, we also have had to give up some of our independence and become more dependent on family and friends. We learn the gift of interdependence when we learn a balance between the times we can be dependent and when we can be independent. This is not an easy thing for us to do, especially in a society that encourages independence rather than interdependence.

Reading: The Healing of a Paralyzed Man (Luke 5:18–26)

Some men came, carrying a paralyzed man on a bed. They were trying to bring him in and lay him before Jesus; but finding no way to bring him in because of the crowd, they went up on the roof and let him down with his bed through the tiles into the middle of the crowd in front of Jesus. When he saw their faith, he said, "Friend, your sins are forgiven you." Then the scribes and the Pharisees began to question, "Who is this who is speaking blasphemies? Who can forgive sins but God alone?" When Jesus perceived their questionings, he answered them, "Why do you raise such questions in your hearts? Which is easier, to say, 'Your sins are forgiven you,' or to say, 'Stand up and walk'? But so that you may know that the Son of Man has authority on earth to forgive sins"—he said to the one who was paralyzed—"I say to you, stand up and take your bed and go to your home." Immediately he stood up before them, took what he had been lying on, and went to his home, glorifying God. Amazement seized all of them, and they glorified God and were filled with awe, saying, "We have seen strange things today."

Questions on the Scripture Passage

- What do friends of the paralyzed man do for him?
- Why, do you think, are the Pharisees and scribes unable to believe?
- What does the paralyzed man do after he is forgiven and healed?

Personal Questions

- What are some ways in which you have lost independence?
- How have you become more interdependent?
- What are some blessings in becoming more interdependent?

Petitions

For the wisdom of balancing dependence and independence in our lives, we pray . . .

That we as a faith community will be more trusting of one another, God, and ourselves, we pray . . .

(Add your own intentions.)

Concluding Prayer

Compassionate God, help us, like this paralyzed man and his friends, to be more trusting of all that you have promised us. Help us to reach out in faith to aid others. And help us to ask for assistance when we need it, especially as we grow older. Amen.

Additional resource. *Aging Gracefully,* by Adrian Van Kaam et al. (Saint Paul Books and Media).

Golfing with Friends

What is revealed to us as we ride or walk the fairways and greens of a golf course to compete with others and ourselves? The activity, serenity, scenery, and time spent with friends are all invaluable. The feelings of being on par, birdieing or acing a hole, and meeting a challenge are terrific. Golfing is a wholesome experience of friendship, of the beauty of God's creation, of our competitive spirit, and of enjoyable exercise. Many aspects of life reveal themselves to us as we play.

Reading: A Samaritan Woman (John 4:6–26)

Jesus, tired out by his journey, was sitting by the well. It was about noon.

A Samaritan woman came to draw water, and Jesus said to her, "Give me a drink." . . . The Samaritan woman said to him, "How is it that you, a Jew, ask a drink of me, a woman of Samaria?" . . . Jesus answered her, "If you knew the gift of God, and who it is that is saying to you, 'Give me a drink,' you would have asked him, and he would have given you living water." The woman said to him, "Sir, you have no bucket, and the well is deep. Where do you get that living water? Are you greater than our ancestor Jacob, who gave us the well, and with his sons and his flocks drank from it?" Jesus said to her, "Everyone who drinks of this water will be thirsty again, but those who drink of the water that I will give them will never be thirsty. The water that I will give will become in them a spring of water gushing up to eternal life." The woman said to him, "Sir, give me this water, so that I may never be thirsty or have to keep coming here to draw water."

Jesus said to her, "Go, call your husband, and come back." The woman answered him, "I have no husband." Jesus said to her, "You are right in saying, 'I have no husband'; for you have had five husbands, and the one you have now is not your husband. What you have said is true!" The woman said to him, "Sir, I see that you are a prophet. Our ancestors worshiped on this mountain, but you say that the place where people must worship is in Jerusalem." Jesus said to her, "Woman, believe me, the hour is coming when you will worship the Father neither on this mountain nor in Jerusalem. You worship what you do not know; we worship what we know, for salvation is from the Jews. But the hour is coming, and is now here, when the true worshipers will worship the Father in spirit and truth, for the Father seeks such as these to worship him. God is spirit, and those who worship him must worship in spirit and truth." The woman said to him, "I know that Messiah is coming" (who is called Christ). "When he comes, he will proclaim all things to us." Jesus said to her, "I am he, the one who is speaking to you."

Questions on the Scripture Passage

- What is revealed to the woman at the well as she talks to Jesus?
- How does this new understanding of her life change her?
- Do you think the Samaritan woman ever sees or talks to Jesus again, or wants to? Why or why not?

Personal Questions

- What has been revealed to you through another person?
- If you do not golf, you probably have had many times of sharing as in a game of golf. What can you tell others about moments of fun and play you have experienced?
- What has your competitive spirit taught you?

Petitions

For family and friends who have walked the journey of life with us, we pray . . .

For those who teach us the joys of living, we pray . . .

(Add your own intentions.)

Concluding Prayer

Our Creator, we know that you send people into our lives to give us insights into who we are. Jesus taught such a lesson to the Samaritan woman as they talked. Help us to see the joy that people bring to us as we compete, live, and experience the revelation of God to us, even in our play. Amen.

Suggested action. Play a round of golf or any other game that you enjoy with friends.

Prayer Life

In simple terms, prayer is being aware of God's presence and responding to that awareness. Certainly prayer can be a source of comfort for us. It can calm our busy life. We pray for ourselves and others. We offer our day to God, thankful for another twenty-four hours of living. Sometimes in our distractions, we forget to pray. But even then we know that God will always be with us.

Reading: Prayer for Disciples and Believers (John 17:7–14, NAB)

Now they know that everything you gave me is from you, because the words you gave to me I have given to them, and they accepted them and truly understood that I came from you, and they have believed that you sent me. I pray for them. I do not pray for the world but for the ones you have given me, because they are yours, and everything of mine is yours and everything of yours is mine, and I have been glorified in them. And now I will no longer be in the world, but they are in the world, while I am coming to you. Holy Father, keep them in your name that you have given me, so that they may be one just as we are. When I was with them I protected them in your name that you gave me, and I guarded them, and none of them was lost except the son of destruction, in order that the scripture might be fulfilled. But now I am coming to you. I speak this in the world so that they may share my joy completely. I gave them your word, and the world hated them, because they do not belong to the world any more than I belong to the world.

Questions on the Scripture Passage

- Why, do you think, does Jesus pray to God for those who will follow him?
- Jesus prays that all may be one. What do you think that means?
- How does Jesus live on in us?

Personal Questions

- How and when do you pray?
- Do you make time to discover God?
- Do you ever feel a sense of God's presence in your parish community?
- What can you share about a time when prayer made a difference in your life?

Petitions

For those who have asked us to pray for them and their intentions, we pray . . .

For the intentions of our parish community, we pray . . .

(Add your own intentions.)

Concluding Prayer

Ever present God, we know that we are to pray for ourselves and others. Free us from our fears. Help us discover the anchor of hope you are for us when we pray to you. Amen.

Additional resource. *Praying Our Experiences,* by Joseph F. Schmidt (Saint Mary's Press).

Family Gatherings

Family gatherings are wonderful events. They let us see one another and share stories about the living as well as the dead. All the new babies and young children give us the feeling that we live on and on. Another marvelous part of the experience is preparing and eating food together. Sometimes families travel all across the country just to get together. How good it is being with one another laughing, crying, and remembering! These gatherings provide us with the opportunity to step back and be grateful for the people in our families who pass on to us our traditions and stories.

Reading: The Wedding at Cana (John 2:1–11)

There was a wedding in Cana of Galilee, and the mother of Jesus was there. Jesus and his disciples had also been invited to the wedding. When the wine gave out, the mother of Jesus said to him, "They have no wine." And Jesus said to her, "Woman, what concern is that to you and to me? My hour has not yet come." His mother said to the servants, "Do whatever he tells you." Now standing there were six stone water jars for the Jewish rites of purification, each holding twenty or thirty gallons. Jesus said to them, "Fill the jars with water." And they filled them up to the brim. He said to them, "Now draw some out, and take it to the chief steward." So they took it. When the steward tasted the water that had become wine, and did not know where it came from (though the servants who had drawn the water knew), the steward called the bridegroom and said to him, "Everyone serves the good wine first, and then the inferior wine after the guests have become drunk. But you have kept the good wine until now." Jesus did this, the first of his signs, in Cana of Galilee, and revealed his glory; and his disciples believed in him.

Questions on the Scripture Passage

- Do you think Jesus likes to party and go to family celebrations?
- Do you think that when Mary tells Jesus there is no wine, she understands what Jesus will do?
- Why do the Scriptures include this story?

Personal Questions

- What can you tell about some of your favorite family gatherings?
- Can you share a story about your wedding or someone else's?
- What do you remember about a favorite grandparent, aunt, or uncle and why he or she is special?

Petitions

For a greater appreciation of family and the strengthening of all families, we pray . . .

For the grandparents or other family members who made us feel special, we pray . . .

(Add your own intentions.)

Concluding Prayer

Loving God, we ask that you stay near our family members, both living and dead. Help us to remember the wonderful times we have had together. Bless our efforts as families to do the best we can with the knowledge and faith we have in you. We ask this prayer in Jesus' name. Amen.

Additional resource. *Family Spirituality: The Raw Ingredients of Faith,* by Leif Kehrwald (ACTA Publications).

Forgiveness

Often in our relationships we need to say we are sorry for something we wish we had not said or done. Many times, too, others do or say something that causes them to ask us for forgiveness. Probably the hardest people to forgive are close family members and ourselves. But sharing our weaknesses and forgiving one another can deepen and strengthen our relationships. Not forgiving punishes us over and over.

Reading: The Unforgiving Servant (Matthew 18:21–35)

Then Peter came and said to him, "Lord, if another member of the church sins against me, how often should I forgive? As many as seven times?" Jesus said to him, "Not seven times, but, I tell you, seventy-seven times.

"For this reason the kingdom of heaven may be compared to a king who wished to settle accounts with his slaves. When he began the reckoning, one who owed him ten thousand talents was brought to him; and, as he could not pay, his lord ordered him to be sold, together with his wife and children and all his possessions, and payment to be made. So the slave fell on his knees before him, saying, 'Have patience with me, and I will pay you everything.' And out of pity for him, the lord of that slave released him and forgave him the debt. But that same slave, as he went out, came upon one of his fellow slaves who owed him a hundred denarii; and seizing him by the throat, he said, 'Pay what you owe.' Then his fellow slave fell down and pleaded with him, 'Have patience with me, and I will pay you.' But he refused; then he went and threw him into prison until he would pay the debt. When his fellow slaves saw what had happened, they were greatly distressed, and they went and reported to their lord all that had taken place. Then his lord summoned him and said to him, 'You wicked slave! I forgave you all that debt because you pleaded with me. Should you not have had mercy on your fellow slave, as I had mercy on you?' And in anger his lord handed him over to be tortured until he would pay his entire debt. So my heavenly Father will also do to every one of you, if you do not forgive your brother or sister from your heart."

Questions on the Scripture Passage

- How often does Jesus ask us to forgive? Is this asking too much?
- Does the first slave experience "real" forgiveness? Why, do you think, can he not give this same forgiveness to his fellow slave?
- What do you think it means to forgive from the heart?

Personal Questions

- Have you ever been moved to be merciful and forgive someone?
- Have you ever been forgiven?
- Have you forgiven from your heart? If so, what was that like?
- What is the difference between forgiving and forgetting?

Petitions

For the courage to reach out in forgiveness, we pray . . .

That we will accept the forgiveness offered to us, we pray . . .

(Add your own intentions.)

Concluding Prayer

Merciful God, you have asked us to forgive seventy-seven times, for you know how much we as humans fail and need forgiveness. Keep us ever willing to reach out and forgive from the heart both ourselves and others. Amen.

Additional resources. *The Hurt,* by Teddi Doleski (Paulist Press).

The Velveteen Rabbit, by Margery Williams Bianco (Avon Books; also available from other publishers).

Mary, One of Us

Mary the mother of Christ Jesus is a model for us in the church. She exemplifies openness to God's will. She trusts the spirit of God working in her life. She is courageous in the face of suffering and, above all, faithful and generous with her simple yes to God.

Reading: The Announcement of the Birth of Jesus (Luke 1:26–38)

In the sixth month the angel Gabriel was sent by God to a town in Galilee called Nazareth, to a virgin engaged to a man whose name was Joseph, of the house of David. The virgin's name was Mary. And he came to her and said, "Greetings, favored one! The Lord is with you." But she was much perplexed by his words and pondered what sort of greeting this might be. The angel said to her, "Do not be afraid, Mary, for you have found favor with God. And now, you will conceive in your womb and bear a son, and you will name him Jesus. He will be great, and will be called the Son of the Most High, and the Lord God will give to him the throne of his ancestor David. He will reign over the house of Jacob forever, and of his kingdom there will be no end." Mary said to the angel, "How can this be, since I am a virgin?" The angel said to her, "The Holy Spirit will come upon you, and the power of the Most High will overshadow you; therefore the child to be born will be holy; he will be called Son of God. And now, your relative Elizabeth in her old age has also conceived a son; and this is the sixth month for her who was said to be barren. For nothing will be impossible with God." Then Mary said, "Here am I, the servant of the Lord; let it be with me according to your word." Then the angel departed from her.

Questions on the Scripture Passage

- How does this scene in the Scriptures set Mary apart as special and uniquely significant for people even now?
- Does Mary seem to be afraid? Why or why not?
- What is Mary's trusting statement to the angel?

Personal Questions

- When have you felt that God asked something of you?
- Can you think of an important time when you trusted a friend or family member?
- Have you ever turned to Mary for trust or courage?

Petitions

That we may follow the example of the role models who manifest Christ to us, we pray . . .

That Mary may intercede with her Son for us, we pray . . .

(Add your own intentions.)

Concluding Prayer

Mary, help us to acquire many of the qualities you have taught us by your example. Give us courage, wisdom, trust, compassion, faithfulness, and generosity. May we model these qualities for one another. Amen.

Additional resource. *The Ageless Self: Sources of Meaning in Later Life,* by Sharon R. Kaufman (University of Wisconsin Press).

The Loss of a Child

Some of us will outlive our children. They might die of an illness. They might die quickly in a car accident, or they might commit suicide. When they die, they are gone, and we will not see them again. Burying a child is simply the hardest thing in the world to do. As time goes by it may be less painful, or we may feel on occasion that it would be easier to have been the one to die. The fulfillment of hopes and dreams for a deceased child lives on in the parents. The parents carry that child with them forever.

Reading: Crucifixion and Death (John 19:17–30, NAB)

Carrying the cross himself [Jesus] went out to what is called the Place of the Skull, in Hebrew, Golgotha. There they crucified him, and with him two others, one on either side, with Jesus in the middle. Pilate also had an inscription written and put on the cross. It read, "Jesus the Nazorean, the King of the Jews." Now many of the Jews read this inscription, because the place where Jesus was crucified was near the city; and it was written in Hebrew, Latin, and Greek. So the chief priests of the Jews said to Pilate, "Do not write 'The King of the Jews,' but that he said, 'I am the King of the Jews.'" Pilate answered, "What I have written, I have written."

When the soldiers had crucified Jesus, they took his clothes and divided them into four shares, a share for each soldier. They also took his tunic, but the tunic was seamless, woven in one piece from the top down. So they said to one another, "Let's not tear it, but cast lots for it to see whose it will be," in order that the passage of scripture might be fulfilled [that says]:

> "They divided my garments among them,
> and for my vesture they cast lots."

This is what the soldiers did. Standing by the cross of Jesus were his mother and his mother's sister, Mary the wife of Clopas, and Mary of Magdala. When Jesus saw his mother and the disciple there whom he loved, he said to his mother, "Woman, behold, your son." Then he said to the disciple, "Behold, your mother." And from that hour the disciple took her into his home.

After this, aware that everything was now finished, in order that the scripture might be fulfilled, Jesus said, "I thirst." There was a vessel filled with common wine. So they put a sponge soaked in wine on a sprig of hyssop and put it up to his mouth. When Jesus had taken the wine, he said, "It is finished." And bowing his head, he handed over the spirit.

Questions on the Scripture Passage

- Who is with Jesus when he is crucified?
- What does Jesus want those who are there to believe?
- Why, do you think, did the writer of the Gospel story include Jesus' request that John care for Jesus' mother?

Personal Questions

- Has your life been changed by the death of your child or children?

- If you have lost a child, how do or did you deal with the grief, hurt, anger, and pain?
- If you have lost a child, did your faith and hope in God carry you through that experience? If so, how? Did God ever seem distant?
- If a parent who has lost a child came to you for consolation and advice, what would you share with him or her?

Petitions

For parents who have buried a child, we pray . . .

For children who have buried a parent, we pray . . .

(Add your own intentions.)

Concluding Prayer

Holy One, just as Mary and John placed their trust and faith in you, give us the strength and courage to do the same. Especially bless parents who have buried a child. Let them feel your loving presence. Amen.

Additional resource. *Blessed Grieving: Reflections on Life's Losses,* by Joan Guntzelman (Saint Mary's Press).

Developing a Positive Attitude About Aging

Having a positive outlook on aging is a healthy way to grow old in grace, age, and wisdom. Reflecting on what we have done with our lives gives us the hope of living today more fully. Seeing the glass as half full instead of half empty gives life meaning. And we can decide to do that. Troubles are inevitable, but our response is in our hands.

Reading: Living Faith (Isaiah 46:4; 2 Corinthians 4:16–18)

Even to your old age I am he,
even when you turn gray I will carry you.
I have made, and I will bear;
I will carry and will save.

So we do not lose heart. Even though our outer nature is wasting away, our inner nature is being renewed day by day. For this slight momentary affliction is preparing us for an eternal weight of glory beyond all measure, because we look not at what can be seen but at what cannot be seen; for what can be seen is temporary, but what cannot be seen is eternal.

Questions on the Scripture Passages

- In the passage from Isaiah, God makes a promise. What does it mean?

- The passage from Corinthians speaks of what is seen and unseen. What does this passage mean to you?

Personal Questions

- What are some of the gifts of growing old?
- What are some of your gifts and talents that you have shared over the years?
- As you have aged, have you developed new talents?
- Do you have a positive outlook on aging? If so, who or what has helped you develop it?

Petitions

That those who have gone before us in faith may be our guide, we pray . . .

That we may learn from our years of experience to live in age, grace, and wisdom, we pray . . .

(Add your own intentions.)

Concluding Prayer

Creator of the universe, we gain a better and more complete understanding of who we are as we age. Help us to be positive in our aging process and to live fully. Help us to be examples for living in age, grace, and wisdom. Amen.

Additional resource. *Don't Sweat the Small Stuff—and It's All Small Stuff: Simple Ways to Keep the Little Things from Taking Over Your Life,* by Richard Carlson (Hyperion).

Incarnational Moments: God-with-Us

What does it mean for us to wait for Jesus to come again into our heart? We know he came in human history, once and for all. Each Advent we prepare to celebrate the coming of Jesus, but in truth, Jesus is here with us every day. Our relationship with Jesus deepens as we listen, grow, and are open to insights that change our life and that give us incarnational moments in which God reveals who God is for us. We just have to keep our eyes, ears, and heart open.

Reading: The Transfiguration of Jesus (Matthew 17:1–8)

Six days later, Jesus took with him Peter and James and his brother John and led them up a high mountain, by themselves. And he was transfigured before them, and his face shone like the sun, and his clothes became dazzling white. Suddenly there appeared to them Moses and Elijah, talking with him. Then Peter said to Jesus, "Lord, it is good for us to be here; if you wish, I will make three dwellings here, one for you, one for Moses, and one for Elijah." While he was still speaking, suddenly a bright cloud overshadowed them, and from the cloud a voice said, "This is my Son, the Beloved; with him I am well pleased; listen to him!" When the disciples heard this, they fell to the ground and were overcome by fear. But Jesus came and touched them, saying, "Get up and do not be afraid." And when they looked up, they saw no one except Jesus himself alone.

Questions on the Scripture Passage

- What do you think Peter, James, and John feel and think when Jesus is transfigured before them?
- When God says, "This is my Son, the Beloved," would you have been fearful like the disciples?
- Why does Jesus encourage the disciples to let go of their fear?

Personal Questions

- Who is the Jesus you knew when you were young?
- Who is, or was, the Jesus of your working years?
- Have you ever for a second seen the face of Jesus in someone you knew? In what other moments have you recognized God-with-you?

Petitions

That we will always appreciate God's becoming one of us, we pray . . .

That we will see in others and ourselves the image and likeness of God, we pray . . .

(Add your own intentions.)

Concluding Prayer

Ever present, loving God, help us to know we are made in your image and likeness. As we remember Jesus' coming to be one of us, help us to discover deeper insights into your working in our everyday lives. Amen.

Additional resource. *Affirmative Aging: A Creative Approach to Longer Life,* edited by Joan E. Lukens (Morehouse Publishing).

Caregivers

Relationships call most of us to be caregivers. Maybe a parent, a brother or sister, a child, a spouse, or a friend has needed or will need our support. We never know when we will be summoned to serve another. When we are caregivers we may sometimes want to rest at the feet of Jesus. Fortunately, God invites us to ask for the help we need in order to do the best we can.

Reading: Martha and Mary (Luke 10:38–42)

Now as they went on their way, he entered a certain village, where a woman named Martha welcomed him into her home. She had a sister named Mary, who sat at the Lord's feet and listened to what he was saying. But Martha was distracted by her many tasks; so she came to him and asked, "Lord, do you not care that my sister has left me to do all the work by myself? Tell her then to help me." But the Lord answered her, "Martha, Martha, you are worried and distracted by many things; there is need of only one thing. Mary has chosen the better part, which will not be taken away from her."

Questions on the Scripture Passage

- What does Mary want to do? Why?
- What does Martha want Mary to do? Why?
- What does Jesus tell Martha? Do you agree?

Personal Questions

- Are you more like Martha or Mary? Explain.
- How have you been a caregiver?
- Have you ever been the person cared for?
- What blessings are there in being a caregiver? being the one cared for?
- What do you do when you feel anger, hurt, or fear?

Petitions

For all those who are caring for sick or elderly people, we pray . . .

For all who are cared for by someone else, we pray . . .

(Add your own intentions.)

Concluding Prayer

Divine Caregiver, take care of and bless all who give of themselves to care for another. Let us know that it is okay to feel anger, fear, and hurt when our caregiving seems unappreciated. Help us to do the best we can and to place our trust in you. Amen.

Additional resource. *Caring: How Can We Love One Another?* by Morton T. Kelsey (Paulist Press).

columba

Review Slip

Title Wisdom Keepers

Subtitle A Resource for Faith Sharing Among Seniors

Author Sharan A. Benton

ISBN 0 88489 626 9

Price £6.99stg / IR£8.50

Extent 135pp

Publisher Saint Mary's Press

For further information contact:
Brian Lynch,
PR & Marketing Manager,
Columba, 55A Stillorgan Industrial Park, Blackrock,
Co Dublin, Ireland.
Tel + 353 1 294 2556 Mobile + 353 86 8214842
Fax + 353 1 294 2564 Email brian@columba.ie

Ice Cream

Have you ever stopped to think about your sweet tooth? It's a fun tooth! It gives us a chance to eat ice cream with all the people who love that treat. If we are shopping with friends, sometimes it's nice to reward ourselves with the pleasure of ice cream. Part of the fun of eating ice cream can be learning what we like best by making choices and trying something different each time. Eating ice cream is one experience we like to share with others because it lightens our hearts. Having simple pleasurable moments is a gift we might need more of.

READING: THE HYMN OF A GRATEFUL HEART (PSALM 138)

I give you thanks, O LORD, with my whole heart;
before the gods I sing your praise;
I bow down toward your holy temple
and give thanks to your name for your steadfast love
and your faithfulness;
for you have exalted your name and your word
above everything.
On the day I called, you answered me,
you increased my strength of soul.

All the kings of the earth shall praise you, O LORD,
for they have heard the words of your mouth.
They shall sing of the ways of the LORD,
for great is the glory of the LORD.

For though the LORD is high, he regards the lowly;
  but the haughty he perceives from far away.

Though I walk in the midst of trouble,
  you preserve me against the wrath of my enemies;
you stretch out your hand,
  and your right hand delivers me.
The LORD will fulfill his purpose for me;
  your steadfast love, O LORD, endures forever.
  Do not forsake the work of your hands.

Questions on the Scripture Passage

- What does the psalm say about being grateful?
- Why is it important to be grateful to God?
- How is gratitude a powerful force against pain, trouble, doubt, and suffering?

Personal Questions

- What does your sweet tooth like the best?
- How do you thank others?
- Would it be helpful to make a list of everything you are grateful for, and then pull it out and offer it to God, especially when life is difficult?
- Who is your favorite person to take for ice cream?

Petitions

For the people who help us to be thankful to God, we pray . . .

For the times we asked for strawberry ice cream and got chocolate, we pray . . .

(Add your own intentions.)

Concluding Prayer

Loving Creator of all that is good, may we have hearts that are grateful to the people who do so many things for us. Help us to be joyful and playful when we share ice cream and good times with those we care about. May we make it a habit always to say thank you to one another and to you, our God. Amen.

Suggested action. Take someone you love for ice cream and satisfy that sweet tooth.

Giving Up Activities We Always Enjoyed

Some of the activities that we used to do so easily and so well, we can no longer do. Maybe we sewed, or baked, or played tennis, or worked on our car, or enjoyed arts and crafts, or traveled, or cared for children, or loved to shop. We may have had to give up a favorite activity at this time in our life. A certain amount of grieving comes with relinquishing dear pastimes. So, we pray for letting go.

READING: THE STORY OF EMMAUS (LUKE 24:13–31)

Now on that same day two of [Jesus' disciples] were going to a village called Emmaus . . . and talking with each other about all these things that had happened. While they were talking and discussing, Jesus himself came near and went with them, but their eyes were kept from recognizing him. And he said to them, "What are you discussing with each other while you walk along?" . . . They replied, "The things [that have taken place] about Jesus of Nazareth, . . . and how our chief priests and leaders handed him over to be condemned to death and crucified him. But we had hoped that he was the one to redeem Israel. Yes, and besides all this, it is now the third day since these things took place. Moreover, some women of our group astounded us. They were at the tomb early this morning, and when they did not find his body there, they came back and told us that they had indeed seen a vision of angels who said that he was alive. Some of those who were with us went to the tomb and found it just as the women had said; but they did not see him." Then he said to them, "Oh, how foolish you are, and how slow of heart to believe all that the prophets have declared! Was it not necessary that the Messiah should suffer these things and then enter into his glory?" Then beginning with Moses and all the prophets, he interpreted to them the things about himself in all the scriptures.

As they came near the village to which they were going, he walked ahead as if he were going on. But they urged him strongly, saying, "Stay with us, because it is almost evening and the day is now nearly over." So he went in to stay with them. When he was at the table with them, he took bread, blessed and broke it, and gave it to them. Then their eyes were opened, and they recognized him; and he vanished from their sight.

Questions on the Scripture Passage

- What do these disciples say to Jesus on the way to Emmaus?
- How does Jesus accept them where they are, but still teach them and expand their perceptions?
- What do the disciples have to give up before they can recognize Jesus?

Personal Questions

- What have you had to give up in recent years?
- How hard is it to let go of the things you once did?
- What are you doing now that you did not have time for when you were younger?
- Do you believe that doing less does not make you less? Explain.

Petitions

That we may let go of the things we can no longer do, we pray . . .

That we may find creative activities that continue to give life energy and joy, we pray . . .

(Add your own intentions.)

Concluding Prayer

Loving God, teach us the wisdom of not having to do everything. Let us turn some things that we can no longer do over to you. Help us to find new and meaningful things that help us to touch others' lives as well as our own. Amen.

Additional resource. *Disgracefully Yours: More New Ideas for Getting the Most Out of Life,* by the Hen Co-op (Crossing Press).

Pets

Dogs, cats, and birds—our pets—can play an important part in our lives. Our pets can be a comfort to us. Our dog greets us when we come in, tail wagging, happy to see us. Our cat follows us to be where we are, wanting to curl up in our lap. We develop lasting relationships as we care for our pets and they care for us. The deaths of our pets bring a heavy loss. We grieve for them as we do for lost friends. Nevertheless, fond memories remind us of the gifts. Let us always celebrate our pets.

Reading: Preparation for the Flood (Genesis 6:14–21)

Make yourself an ark of cypress wood; make rooms in the ark, and cover it inside and out with pitch. This is how you are to make it: the length of the ark three hundred cubits, its width fifty cubits, and its height thirty cubits. Make a roof for the ark, and finish it to a cubit above; and put the door of the ark in its side; make it with lower, second, and third decks. For my part, I am going to bring a flood of waters on the earth, to destroy from under heaven all flesh in which is the breath of life; everything that is on the earth shall die. But I will establish my covenant with you; and you shall come into the ark, you, your sons, your wife, and your sons' wives with you. And of every living thing, of all flesh, you shall bring two of every kind into the ark, to keep them alive with you; they shall be male and female. Of the birds according to their kinds, and of the animals according to their kinds, of every creeping thing of the ground according to its kind, two of every kind shall come in to you, to keep them alive. Also take with you every kind of food that is eaten, and store it up; and it shall serve as food for you and for them.

Questions on the Scripture Passage

- Why, do you think, is it important to God to make a covenant with Noah and his family?
- Why, do you think, are the animals put on the ark?
- How are Noah and his family to care for the animals?

Personal Questions

- Have you ever had a family pet that meant a great deal to you? If so, what stories come to mind about this animal?
- Has a family pet died? If so, how hard was that?
- What advice would you give to a first-time pet owner?
- How do pets reflect God's love for us?

Petitions

For all families that have animals that add much pleasure to their lives, we pray . . .

For the beauty of all animals, both wild and tame, we pray . . .

(Add your own intentions.)

Concluding Prayer

Creator of all creatures great and small, you have blessed us with the beauty of the birds and the beasts. All these give us much joy and pleasure. Thank you, God, for the gift of animals. Amen.

Additional resource. *Bless the Beasts: A Spirituality of Animal Care,* by Jeffrey G. Sobosan (Crossroad Publishing Co.).

Calming Stormy Seas

At times we face the stormy seas of disapproval, anger, misunderstanding, or fear. Occasionally we get upset with ourselves and think that we have done something to bring up the storm. Probably the key is staying calm, trusting the storm will pass. Sometimes we are called to walk through the storm with others. Other times we need to be a calming presence.

Reading: The Calming of the Sea (Mark 4:35–41)

On that day, when evening had come, [Jesus] said to them, "Let us go across to the other side." And leaving the crowd behind, they took him with them in the boat, just as he was. Other boats were with him. A great windstorm arose, and the waves beat into the boat, so that the boat was already being swamped. But he was in the stern, asleep on the cushion; and they woke him up and said to him, "Teacher, do you not care that we are perishing?" He woke up and rebuked the wind, and said to the sea, "Peace! Be still!" Then the wind ceased, and there was a dead calm. He said to them, "Why are you afraid? Have you still no faith?" And they were filled with great awe and said to one another, "Who then is this, that even the wind and the sea obey him?"

Questions on the Scripture Passage

- What feelings are the disciples experiencing?
- What is Jesus' response to the disciples?
- What is Jesus teaching us in this story?

Personal Questions

- Experiences that upset us in our youth many times do not upset us in our later years. Why?
- What do you do to calm yourself when you feel afraid?
- What important lesson have you learned about fears and coping with them?

Petitions

For the times we fear that God will not take care of us, we pray . . .

For the courage to trust in God, we pray . . .

(Add your own intentions.)

Concluding Prayer

Merciful God, you know at times we are frightened. Help us to remain calm and trust that you will be with us during the storms of our life. Thank you for the times we know we will not perish because you are with us. Amen.

Additional resource. *A Deepening Love Affair: The Gift of Love in Later Life,* by Jane Marie Thibault (Upper Room Books).

The Loss of a Friend

At some time during our life we will lose a friend in death. As we get older, losses like the death of a childhood friend, a high school buddy, a person at church, or a friend of the family become more frequent. In each case, because we and that person have shared so much of our lives, both good and bad, we truly miss her or him. Because we have loved and been loved, we are changed by that death.

Reading: Mary Magdalene at the Tomb (Mark 16:1–11)

When the sabbath was over, Mary Magdalene, and Mary the mother of James, and Salome bought spices, so that they might go and anoint him. And very early on the first day of the week, when the sun had risen, they went to the tomb. They had been saying to one another, "Who will roll away the stone for us from the entrance to the tomb?" When they looked up, they saw that the stone, which was very large, had already been rolled back. As they entered the tomb, they saw a young man, dressed in a white robe, sitting on the right side; and they were alarmed. But he said to them, "Do not be alarmed; you are looking for Jesus of Nazareth, who was crucified. He has been raised; he is not here. Look, there is the place they laid him. But go, tell his disciples and Peter that he is going ahead of you to

Galilee; there you will see him, just as he told you." So they went out and fled from the tomb, for terror and amazement had seized them; and they said nothing to anyone, for they were afraid.

Now after he rose early on the first day of the week, he appeared first to Mary Magdalene, from whom he had cast out seven demons. She went out and told those who had been with him, while they were mourning and weeping. But when they heard that he was alive and had been seen by her, they would not believe it.

Questions on the Scripture Passage

- Why do the women go to the tomb?
- What is it like for Mary to recognize Jesus?
- Why is it so hard for the others to believe Jesus rose from the dead?

Personal Questions

- Why are tears a help in coping with the loss of a friend?
- Do you believe we will see our friends again in the next life?
- Do you recognize the resurrected Christ in your life today? If so, how?
- Has the Resurrection helped you grieve the loss of a friend?

Petitions

For all the friends who have loved us, we pray . . .

For the friends we have buried, that they may have eternal life, we pray . . .

(Add your own intentions.)

Concluding Prayer

Living God, we place our trust in you. We believe that we will see again all those who have preceded us into the next life. Strengthen us with your love and comfort as we remember the others who have loved us. Amen.

Additional resource. *Old Friends,* by Tracy Kidder (Houghton Mifflin Co.).

Solitude

Where do you go when you want to have some peace? Sometimes we go to a physical place, and sometimes we go within ourselves. We want to sense the peace of which Jesus speaks, the peace that the world cannot give. Going to a place of solitude can take us to our insecurities and fears, as well as to joy and peace. If we can trust that God is with us, we will discover the peace of Christ.

Reading: Joy and Peace (Philippians 4:4–9)

Rejoice in the Lord always; again I will say, Rejoice. Let your gentleness be known to everyone. The Lord is near. Do not worry about anything, but in everything by prayer and supplication with thanksgiving let your requests be made known to God. And the peace of God, which surpasses all understanding, will guard your hearts and your minds in Christ Jesus.

Finally, beloved, whatever is true, whatever is honorable, whatever is just, whatever is pure, whatever is pleasing, whatever is commendable, if there is any excellence and if there is anything worthy of praise, think about these things. Keep on doing the things that you have learned and received and heard and seen in me, and the God of peace will be with you.

Questions on the Scripture Passage

- The Scripture passage tells us to rejoice in God. What does this mean for us, and how do we do it?
- The Scripture passage says that we have peace within us when we do certain things. What are they? Have you seen the truth of this passage?
- There are six "whatevers" that we are to think about. What are they, and what do you feel about them?

Personal Questions

- When do you feel at peace?
- Sometimes we want others to meet our needs, though only Jesus and we can do that. How do you meet your needs?
- Sometimes in solitude we experience insecurities and fears. Has this happened to you?
- Where do you find solitude?

Petitions

That we may reach within to find the peace of Christ, we pray . . .

That our congregations may reach out to those who have become separated from them, we pray . . .

(Add your own intentions.)

Concluding Prayer

Solitude can be a creative place for us to go. Help us, loving God, to let go of our fears and insecurities, so that we truly experience the peace of Christ that the world cannot give. Amen.

Additional resource. *Out of Solitude: Three Meditations on the Christian Life,* by Henri J. M. Nouwen (Ave Maria Press).

Praying the Rosary

The rosary is a traditional Catholic prayer. It offers us the opportunity to reflect on the birth, life, death, and Resurrection of Jesus as we say the Joyful, Sorrowful, and Glorious Mysteries. We reflect on the mysteries to give meaning to our life today and to remember always who Jesus is and who Jesus can be for us now. The rosary is probably not prayed as commonly now as it was twenty or thirty years ago, but it remains a satisfying and meaningful devotion.

Reading: Celebrating Jesus (Philippians 2:2–11)

Make my joy complete: be of the same mind, having the same love, being in full accord and of one mind. Do nothing from selfish ambition or conceit, but in humility regard others as better than yourselves. Let each of you look not to your own interests, but to the interests of others. Let the same mind be in you that was in Christ Jesus,

who, though he was in the form of God,
did not regard equality with God
as something to be exploited,
but emptied himself,
taking the form of a slave,
being born in human likeness.

And being found in human form,
he humbled himself
and became obedient to the point of death—
even death on a cross.

Therefore God also highly exalted him
and gave him the name
that is above every name,
so that at the name of Jesus
every knee should bend,
in heaven and on earth and under the earth,
and every tongue should confess
that Jesus Christ is Lord,
to the glory of God.

Questions on the Scripture Passage

- What does it mean to have the mind of Christ?
- As you consider the mysteries of the birth, death, Resurrection, and Ascension of Jesus, what do your reflections suggest about Mary?
- How is God at work in you, especially when you pray the rosary?

Personal Questions

- What does saying the rosary mean to you?
- How do you feel when you pray the rosary?
- If you have not prayed the rosary in a while, what do you think about trying it again?

Petitions

For all mothers who have nurtured children, we pray . . .

That we may let God work in us so that Christ's mind can be our mind and Christ's heart be our heart, we pray . . .

(Add your own intentions.)

Concluding Prayer

Hail Mary, full of grace, the Lord is with you; blessed are you among women, and blessed is the fruit of your womb, Jesus. Holy Mary, mother of God, pray for us sinners, now and at the hour of our death. Amen.

Additional resource. *Dogmatic Constitution on the Church* (*Lumen Gentium,* 1964), number 8, from the documents of Vatican Council II.

Giftedness

We sometimes forget the gifts that we have and can bring to others in our older years. We do not take ourselves nearly as seriously as we did in our younger years. We now know that we do not have to like everybody, and we know not everyone likes us. What a gift! We are free to do volunteer work at many places needing our help. We can spoil our grandchildren and then send them home. We can visit the sick, make new friends, and do many of the things we never had time for when we were working or raising children or both. Maybe one of the greatest gifts of being an elder is the wisdom to know that there is a time for everything and that's just the way life is.

READING: THERE IS A TIME (ECCLESIASTES 3:1–15)

For everything there is a season, and a time for every matter under heaven:

a time to be born, and a time to die;
a time to plant, and a time to pluck up what is planted;
a time to kill, and a time to heal;
a time to break down, and a time to build up;
a time to weep, and a time to laugh;
a time to mourn, and a time to dance;
a time to throw away stones, and a time to gather stones together;

a time to embrace, and a time to refrain from
  embracing;
a time to seek, and a time to lose;
a time to keep, and a time to throw away;
a time to tear, and a time to sew;
a time to keep silence, and a time to speak;
a time to love, and a time to hate;
a time for war, and a time for peace.

What gain have the workers from their toil? I have seen the business that God has given to everyone to be busy with. He has made everything suitable for its time; moreover he has put a sense of past and future into their minds, yet they cannot find out what God has done from the beginning to the end. I know that there is nothing better for them than to be happy and enjoy themselves as long as they live; moreover, it is God's gift that all should eat and drink and take pleasure in all their toil. I know that whatever God does endures forever; nothing can be added to it, nor anything taken from it; God has done this, so that all should stand in awe before him. That which is, already has been; that which is to be, already is; and God seeks out what has gone by.

Questions on the Scripture Passage

- How does this Scripture passage match your experience? Do the times of peace and war, and birth and death come out even somehow?
- All of us, the Scripture passage says, want to do well with our life. How have you done that for yourself?
- What do you think the statement "whatever God does will endure forever" means?

Personal Questions

- What gifts have you discovered in yourself as you have aged?
- Have those newly discovered gifts helped you cope with the times of death and birth, and sorrow and joy?
- In what ways have you shared your gifts with others?
- In what organizations (civic or church) have you gotten involved?
- Has it been rewarding for you to be involved?

Petitions

For all the many blessings we receive because we reach out to others, we pray . . .

For organizations that reach out into the community for volunteers to help with the workload, we pray . . .

(Add your own intentions.)

Concluding Prayer

Generous God, you have given us gifts and talents to share. In an appointed time we have done and will do that. Help us be open to giving what we can, when we can. Thanks for the goodness that embracing life gives to both giver and receiver. Amen.

Additional resource. *Called and Gifted for the Third Millennium,* by U.S. Catholic Bishops (United States Catholic Conference).

Driving Less

Driving allows us to be independent. We want to be useful, so we offer to help or pick up others. We want to drive as long as we can. How will we ever do all the things we do now if we stop driving? Can we ever give up driving? Probably not until we have to. It is hard for most of us to give up our keys. How do we reach a balance between dependence and independence, especially when even we suspect that our driving might involve risk?

Reading: The Parable of the Lamp (Matthew 5:14–16; Mark 4:21–25; see also Luke 8:16–18)

[Jesus said:] "You are the light of the world. A city built on a hill cannot be hid. No one after lighting a lamp puts it under the bushel basket, but on the lampstand, and it gives light to all in the house. In the same way, let your light shine before others, so that they may see your good works and give glory to our Father in heaven."

[Jesus] said to them, "Is a lamp brought in to be put under the bushel basket, or under the bed, and not on the lampstand? For there is nothing hidden, except to be disclosed; nor is anything secret, except to come to light. Let anyone with ears to hear listen!" And he said to them, "Pay attention to what you hear; the measure you give will be the measure you get, and still more will be given you. For to those who have, more will be given; and from those who have nothing, even what they have will be taken away."

Questions on the Scripture Passages

- According to Matthew's Gospel, why is it important to let our light shine?
- What is measured in the way we hear?
- How do we give glory to God?

Personal Questions

- What would you be giving up if you could not drive? Maybe you have already done this.
- Why is it important to use our gifts and talents well?
- Why is it hard for us to ask others for a ride?

Petitions

That those who have the opportunity to drive may reach out when there is a need, we pray . . .

That we may have the wisdom to let people help us when we need help, we pray . . .

(Add your own intentions.)

Concluding Prayer

God of wisdom, help us to be wise people, to be independent when we can and to be dependent when we have to. Help us to know that both independence and dependence are just part of living, not good or bad. It is never easy for us to balance these two states, but with your help we can. Amen.

Additional resource. *Enjoy Old Age: A Program of Self-Management,* by B. F. Skinner and M. E. Vaughan (W. W. Norton and Co.).

Enjoying the Arts

Supporting the arts in our cities and towns is a wonderful gift. The arts give us personal insights into our life experience, deepen our relationships, and help us remain attached to the full range of human emotion. Whether we go to a stage play, a country music show, an orchestra concert, an opera or ballet, or a museum, we know that we will be enriched. Many retired persons support the arts not only by making contributions, but also by attending performances and exhibitions. Some volunteer to be ushers or help in other ways.

Reading: True Riches (Matthew 6:19–34)

[Jesus said,] "Do not store up for yourselves treasures on earth, where moth and rust consume and where thieves break in and steal; but store up for yourselves treasures in heaven, where neither moth nor rust consumes and where thieves do not break in and steal. For where your treasure is, there your heart will be also. . . .

"No one can serve two masters; for a slave will either hate the one and love the other, or be devoted to the one and despise the other. You cannot serve God and wealth.

"Therefore I tell you, do not worry about your life, what you will eat or what you will drink, or about your body, what you will wear. Is not life more than food, and the body more than clothing? Look at the birds of the air; they neither sow nor reap nor gather into barns, and yet your heavenly Father feeds them. Are you not of more value than they? And can any of you by worrying add a single hour to your span of life? . . . Therefore do not worry, saying, 'What will we eat?' or 'What will we drink?' or 'What will we wear?' . . . your heavenly Father knows that you need all these things. But strive first for the kingdom of God and his righteousness, and all these things will be given to you as well.

"So do not worry about tomorrow, for tomorrow will bring worries of its own. Today's trouble is enough for today."

Questions on the Scripture Passage

- How does God take care of the birds of the air?
- What lesson is the Gospel of Matthew teaching us about heavenly treasures?
- Why is Jesus telling us not to worry?
- How are the arts a way of enjoying God's creation too, and part of not worrying?

Personal Questions

- What do concerts, museums, plays, or musicals do for your spirit?
- If you volunteer as a docent or usher or otherwise participate in art events, how has this enriched your life?
- What worries you? How does trusting in God help you to worry less? How can the arts help?

Petitions

For artists who enrich our lives and open our minds to see the world differently, we pray . . .

That we may have the courage to trust in God, we pray . . .

(Add your own intentions.)

Concluding Prayer

God, creator of all, help us to remember the birds of the air. Just as you care for them, we trust that you will care for us. Help us to know that worry often does not have a value, and to believe the message of Jesus that you will always take care of us. May we appreciate your creative power as we appreciate works of art, because you are the source of all creativity. Amen.

Suggested action. Go to a play or to an orchestra performance with a friend, or read a play with others, each of you taking one or more parts.

Mary of Bethany

Mary of Bethany anoints the feet of Jesus and wipes them dry with her hair. The example Mary gives Jesus is a lesson for us in how we are to serve one another. Jesus teaches the disciples the same lesson at the Last Supper when he washes their feet and wipes them with a piece of his own clothing. The disciples are to go and do likewise, and so are we. Loving service is a gift we are called to offer whether young or old, vigorous or frail. Being of service is life-giving to the giver and the receiver.

Reading: The Penitent Woman (Luke 7:37–50)

A woman in the city, who was a sinner, having learned that [Jesus] was eating in the Pharisee's house, brought an alabaster jar of ointment. She stood behind him at his feet, weeping, and began to bathe his feet with her tears and to dry them with her hair. Then she continued kissing his feet and anointing them with the ointment. Now when the Pharisee who had invited him saw it, he said to himself, "If this man were a prophet, he would have known who and what kind of woman this is who is touching him—that she is a sinner." Jesus spoke up and said to him, "Simon, I have something to say to you." "Teacher," he replied, "Speak." "A certain creditor had two debtors; one owed five hundred denarii, and the other fifty. When they could not pay, he canceled the debts for both of them. Now which of them will love him more?" Simon answered, "I suppose the one for whom he canceled the greater debt." And Jesus said to him, "You have judged rightly." Then turning toward the woman, he said to Simon, "Do you see this woman? I entered your house; you gave me no water for my feet, but she has bathed my feet with her tears and dried them with her hair. You gave me no kiss, but from the time I came in she has not stopped kissing my feet. You did not anoint my head with oil, but she has anointed my feet with ointment. Therefore, I tell you, her sins, which were many, have been forgiven; hence she has shown great love. But the one to whom little is forgiven, loves little." Then he said to her, "Your sins are forgiven." But those who were at the table with him began to say among themselves, "Who is this who even forgives sins?" And he said to the woman, "Your faith has saved you; go in peace."

Questions on the Scripture Passage

- Do you think it matters to Jesus that Mary is a sinner? Why or why not?
- Mary offers what she can in service. What is Jesus' reaction?
- What do you think is the message Jesus wants to convey to the Pharisees?

Personal Questions

- How do you serve your family, neighborhood, congregation, or community?
- Do you experience ministry as service?
- How have you grown because of service?

Petitions

That we may follow Jesus' and Mary's examples of loving service, we pray . . .

That the example of service set by Christians throughout history may encourage us, in our faith, to serve as well, we pray . . .

(Add your own intentions.)

Concluding Prayer

Mary is an example to Jesus, Jesus is an example to the disciples, and we are to be examples to one another. Compassionate God, strengthen our faith in and love for you so that we may serve as others have served. Amen.

Additional resource. *Woman, First Among the Faithful,* by Francis J. Moloney (Ave Maria Press).

Front Porch Swings

Many people have spent time sitting on front porch swings or front steps. People sit out front and talk, and watch others washing their cars, children riding bikes, friends checking on neighbors, and individuals trimming and planting and otherwise busy with yard work. At least for part of the year, we are able to experience our neighborhoods from our front porches. But front porch sitting is becoming a lost art for many of us whose lives are far too busy. And new houses seldom even have front porches. Maybe we are missing a lot by not observing and being active in our neighborhoods. We could be missing God working in the everyday life around us. We should know that we can be good neighbors even in a world without front porch swings.

Reading: The Presentation in the Temple (Luke 2:25–40, NAB)

Now there was a man in Jerusalem whose name was Simeon. This man was righteous and devout, awaiting the consolation of Israel, and the holy Spirit was upon him. It had been revealed to him by the holy Spirit that he should not see death before he had seen the Messiah of the Lord. He came in the Spirit into the temple; and when the parents brought in the child Jesus to perform the custom of the law in regard to him, he took him into his arms and blessed God, saying:

"Now, Master, you may let your servant go
in peace, according to your word,
for my eyes have seen your salvation,
which you prepared in sight of all the peoples,
a light for revelation to the Gentiles,
and glory for your people Israel."

The child's father and mother were amazed at what was said about him; and Simeon blessed them and said to Mary his mother, "Behold, this child is destined for the fall and rise of many in Israel, and to be a sign that will be contradicted (and you yourself a sword will pierce) so that the thoughts of many hearts may be revealed." There was also a prophetess, Anna. . . . She was advanced in years, having lived seven years with her husband after her marriage, and then as a widow until she was eighty-four. She never left the temple, but worshiped night and day with fasting and prayer. And coming forward at that very time, she gave thanks to God and spoke about the child to all who were awaiting the redemption of Jerusalem.

When they had fulfilled all the prescriptions of the law of the Lord, they returned to Galilee, to their own town of Nazareth. The child grew and became strong, filled with wisdom; and the favor of God was upon him.

Questions on the Scripture Passage

- Simeon seems to be waiting to see Jesus. What are his words of blessing, and what do you think those words mean?
- How do Simeon and Anna know that Jesus is the one for whom they are waiting?
- How do Simeon and Anna teach us about being hospitable and neighborly?

Personal Questions

- Do you have a neighbor who is also a friend? If so, what do the two of you share together?
- How do you see God revealed in your neighborhood?
- How can you be an even better neighbor?

Petitions

That we may recognize God working in our lives through others, we pray . . .

For those who look in on their neighbors, especially neighbors who are older, we pray . . .

(Add your own intentions.)

Concluding Prayer

God, you reveal yourself both in times past and in times present. Help us to look for you and find your presence in our everyday lives. The pace of life is so fast at times that we can miss your presence with us. Help us to look for you through the eyes of Simeon and Anna. Amen.

Additional resource. *A Saint on Every Corner: Glimpses of Holiness Beyond the Monastery,* by Albert Holtz (Ave Maria Press).

Relating with Our Adult Children

Often our relationships with our adult children become strained—sometimes because we do not communicate, or sometimes because of their or our life choices. Frequently the best we can do for our adult children is to listen: to act as a sounding board and emotional support. They want us to let them live their own lives, but they also want to know that we love them unconditionally. Many of our experiences with our adult children are fun, loving, playful, and wonderful when we relate adult with adult. And we marvel at the adults our children have become.

Reading: The Prodigal Son (Luke 15:11–32)

Jesus said, "There was a man who had two sons. The younger of them said to his father, 'Father, give me the share of the property that will belong to me.' So he divided his property between them. A few days later the younger son gathered all he had and traveled to a distant country, and there he squandered his property in dissolute living. When he had spent everything, a severe famine took place throughout that country, and he began to be in need. So he went and hired himself out to one of the citizens of that country, who sent him to his fields to feed the pigs. He would gladly have filled himself with the pods that the pigs were eating; and no one gave him anything. But when he came to himself he said, 'How many of my father's hired hands have bread enough and to spare, but here I am dying of hunger! I will get up and go to my father, and I will say to him, "Father, I have sinned against heaven and before you; I am no longer worthy to be called your son; treat me like one of your hired hands."' So he set off and went to his father. But while he was still far off, his father saw him and was filled with compassion; he ran and put his arms around him and kissed him. Then the son said to him, 'Father, I have sinned against heaven and before you; I am no longer worthy to be called your son.' But the father said to his slaves, 'Quickly, bring out a robe—the best one—and put it on him; put a ring on his finger and sandals on his feet. And get the fatted calf and kill it, and let us eat and celebrate; for this son of mine was dead and is alive again; he was lost and is found!' And they began to celebrate.

"Now his elder son was in the field; and when he came and approached the house, he heard music and dancing. He called one of the slaves and asked what was going on. He replied, 'Your brother has come, and your father has killed the fatted calf, because he has got him back safe and sound.' Then he became angry and refused to go in. His father came out and began to plead with him. But he answered his father, 'Listen! For all these years I have been working like a slave for you, and I have never disobeyed your command; yet you have never given me even a young goat so that I might celebrate with my friends. But when this son of yours came back, who has devoured your property with prostitutes, you killed the fatted calf for him!' Then the father said to him, 'Son, you are always with me, and all that is mine is yours. But we had to celebrate and rejoice, because this brother of yours was dead and has come to life; he was lost and has been found.'"

Questions on the Scripture Passage

- When the son wants to leave, what does the father do? Why?
- Does the other son understand what the father has done? What do you think of his reaction?
- Who is really more the prodigal (that is, who spends or gives most lavishly): the father or the son?
- What is the parable saying about God's love for us?

Personal Questions

- How does the story of the prodigal son and prodigal father relate to your experience with your adult children?
- What are some ways we can let our children be adults?
- When have you felt most helpful to your adult children?

Petitions

For those who are responsible for children, that they may love those children wisely and well, we pray . . .

For those who struggle with adult children, we pray . . .

(Add your own intentions.)

Concluding Prayer

Our faithful, forgiving God, teach us to learn the wisdom of letting go at some times and of holding on at others. Help us to remember that nothing is impossible with your grace, and help us to share our wisdom, faith, and unconditional love with our children. Amen.

Additional resource. *Grow Old Along with Me—the Best Is Yet to Be,* edited by Sandra Haldeman Martz (Papier-Mache Press).

A Tradition of Faith

Knowing our history as church helps us understand our church today and envision the church of tomorrow. If we know our history and our traditions, and live our faith, we participate in building the church of the future. Learning more about the church can be a lifelong adventure.

Reading: Peter the Rock (Matthew 16:13–20)

Now when Jesus came into the district of Caesarea Philippi, he asked his disciples, "Who do people say that the Son of Man is?" And they said, "Some say John the Baptist, but others Elijah, and still others Jeremiah or one of the prophets." He said to them, "But who do you say that I am?" Simon Peter answered, "You are the Messiah, the Son of the living God." And Jesus answered him, "Blessed are you, Simon son of Jonah! For flesh and blood has not revealed this to you, but my Father in heaven. And I tell you, you are Peter, and on this rock I will build my church, and the gates of Hades will not prevail against it. I will give you the keys of the kingdom of heaven, and whatever you bind on earth will be bound in heaven, and whatever you loose on earth will be loosed in heaven." Then he sternly ordered the disciples not to tell anyone that he was the Messiah.

Questions on the Scripture Passage

- What has God revealed to Simon Peter?
- What do you think it means that Jesus builds the church on the shoulders of human beings like Peter?
- Why, do you think, does Jesus order the disciples not to tell anyone that he is the Messiah?

Personal Questions

- What traditions in the church are important to you?
- How has the church changed in the last thirty years? in your lifetime?
- What are your hopes for the future of the church?

Petitions

For those who have believed in and been faithful to Christ's church, we pray . . .

For those who have left the church and struggle to find God in their lives, we pray . . .

(Add your own intentions.)

Concluding Prayer

We know we live in a very human church, and that Jesus is a witness of who God is for us. Help us to follow the way, the truth, and the life—Jesus—as we witness the church in today's world. Amen.

Additional resource. *Models of Revelation,* by Avery Dulles (Orbis Books).

Appetite Changes

One complaint often shared by people as they age is, "Nothing tastes good." Sometimes the medicine we take affects the taste of food. Sometimes we just do not feel like eating, even when we know we should. And it is generally not fun cooking and eating alone. For many of us, eating was one of our great pleasures in life, and now it has changed. Even so, we can still have a lively appetite for life.

Reading: Zacchaeus the Tax Collector (Luke 19:1–10)

[Jesus] entered Jericho and was passing through it. A man was there named Zacchaeus; he was a chief tax collector and was rich. He was trying to see who Jesus was, but on account of the crowd he could not, because he was short in stature. So he ran ahead and climbed a sycamore tree to see him, because he was going to pass that way. When Jesus came to the place, he looked up and said to him, "Zacchaeus, hurry and come down; for I must stay at your house today." So he hurried down and was happy to welcome him. All who saw it began to grumble and said, "He has gone to be the guest of one who is a sinner." Zacchaeus stood there and said to the Lord, "Look, half of my possessions, Lord, I will give to the poor; and if I have defrauded anyone of anything, I will pay back four times as much." Then Jesus said to him, "Today salvation has come to this house, because he too is a son of Abraham. For the Son of Man came to seek out and to save the lost."

Questions on the Scripture Passage

- Why does Zacchaeus climb the tree?
- Why, do you think, does Jesus want to eat with Zacchaeus?
- Is Zacchaeus a welcoming person with an appetite for new life?

Personal Questions

- Have you ever helped at a soup kitchen? If so, what was that experience like?
- Have your tastes changed lately? If so, how?
- Have you ever taken food to a sick neighbor?
- Do you enjoy eating? Why or why not?
- Whether or not your appetite for food has changed, has your appetite for life remained active? If so, how?

Petitions

For those who have nothing to eat, we pray . . .

For those who invite us to eat with them, we pray . . .

(Add your own intentions.)

Concluding Prayer

Welcoming God, we know that food is a wonderful way to bring people together. You taught us that when you walked this earth. Help us to share food together and take delight in it, both to build up our bodies and to build the Body of Christ. Amen.

Additional resource. *Older and Wiser: 716 Memorable Quotes from Those Who Have Lived the Longest and Seen the Most,* compiled by Gretchen B. Dianda and Betty J. Hofmayer (Ballantine Books).

The Beatitudes

Jesus taught us how to live. The Beatitudes are a way of life for us: they are a guidepost, a rule of thumb, a light in the darkness, a lighthouse. These guidelines help us live out both the Ten Commandments and the commandment of love. The Beatitudes challenge us, but lead to fullness of life. By living them we love as God calls us to love.

Reading: The Sermon on the Mount (Luke 6:20–26)

Then [Jesus] looked up at his disciples and said:

"Blessed are you who are poor,
  for yours is the kingdom of God.
"Blessed are you who are hungry now,
  for you will be filled.
"Blessed are you who weep now,
  for you will laugh.

"Blessed are you when people hate you, and when they exclude you, revile you, and defame you on account of the Son of Man. Rejoice in that day and leap for joy, for surely your reward is great in heaven; for that is what their ancestors did to the prophets.

"But woe to you who are rich,
  for you have received your consolation.
"Woe to you who are full now,
  for you will be hungry.
"Woe to you who are laughing now,
  for you will mourn and weep.

"Woe to you when all speak well of you, for that is what their ancestors did to the false prophets."

Questions on the Scripture Passage

- How will we be blessed?
- What do the woes tell us?
- Jesus came not to abolish the Law but to fulfill the Law. What do you think this means?

Personal Questions

- When have you shown someone mercy?
- What does it feel like to be insulted? Do you feel "blessed" when you are insulted?
- What does being poor in spirit mean to you?
- How do you help bring the Reign of God?

Petitions

For those who have been persecuted and martyred for their faith, we pray . . .

For those who work to bring peace and justice to our world, we pray . . .

(Add your own intentions.)

Concluding Prayer

Source of all peace and justice, help us to show mercy and compassion to your people. Help us to see you in all those we meet. Help us to work toward justice and peace in our world. Bless those who have walked this journey of faith before us. Amen.

Additional resource. *More Random Acts of Kindness,* by the editors of Conari Press (Conari Press).

Financial Wisdom

Juggling finances and changes in lifestyle may challenge us. Retirement may force us to cut back. Additional medical expenses may strain our resources. We learn to do what we can and to trust in the providence of God. Knowing that we will have what we need, though perhaps not all that we want, is really trusting that God will take care of us. We take practical measures with our finances—that's wise; and we invite God to lead us no matter what—that's wise too.

Reading: Trust in God (Luke 12:15–31)

[Jesus said,] "Take care! Be on your guard against all kinds of greed; for one's life does not consist in the abundance of possessions." Then he told them a parable: "The land of a rich man produced abundantly. And he thought to himself, 'What should I do, for I have no place to store my crops?' Then he said, 'I will do this: I will pull down my barns and build larger ones, and there I will store all my grain and my goods. And I will say to my soul, "Soul, you have ample goods laid up for many years; relax, eat, drink, be merry."' But God said to him, 'You fool! This very night your life is being demanded of you. And the things you have prepared, whose will they be?' So it is with those who store up treasures for themselves but are not rich toward God."

He said to his disciples, "Therefore I tell you, do not worry about your life, what you will eat, or about your body, what you will wear. For life is more than food, and the body more than clothing. Consider the ravens: they neither sow nor reap, they have neither storehouse nor barn, and yet God feeds them. Of how much more value are you than the birds! And can any of you by worrying add a single hour to your span of life? If then you are not able to do so small a thing as that, why do you worry about the rest? Consider the lilies, how they grow: they neither toil nor spin; yet I tell you, even Solomon in all his glory was not clothed like one of these. But if God so clothes the grass of the field, which is alive today and tomorrow is thrown into the oven, how much more will he clothe you—you of little faith! And do not keep striving for what you are to eat and what you are to drink, and do not keep worrying. For it is the nations of the world that strive after all these things, and your Father knows that you need them. Instead, strive for his kingdom, and these things will be given to you as well."

Questions on the Scripture Passage

- Jesus speaks of what is important in life. What does he say?
- Does the Scripture passage tell us how to be good stewards?
- How have you trusted in God as this Scripture passage suggests?

Personal Questions

- How are you a good steward?
- Are you blessed when you are generous? If so, how?

- Should we share our resources now or plan to do that when we die?
- Can you recall a time when God's providing for you was apparent?

Petitions

For the times we have doubted that God would take care of us, we pray . . .

For the courage to trust in God's providence while making wise choices about finances, we pray . . .

(Add your own intentions.)

Concluding Prayer

Living God, help us to know that you will take care of us. Just as you took care of us when we were born and throughout our lives until now, so you will take care of us in our later years. Give us the faith to trust in your providence for us. Amen.

Additional resource. *Don't Worry, Make Money: Spiritual and Practical Ways to Create Abundance and More Fun in Your Life,* by Richard Carlson (Hyperion).

Future Church

The people of God, moved by the Spirit and believing in Jesus Christ, come together as a community of worship. We are then sent into the world to serve, love, and make peace. By changing our individual lives and freely using our gifts of loving one another, we transform the world and bring the Reign of God. This transformation is our hope for the future of the church, and all of us have a role in bringing it about.

Reading: Peter's Discourse (Acts of the Apostles 2:14–41)

But Peter, standing with the eleven, raised his voice and addressed them, "Men of Judea and all who live in Jerusalem, let this be known to you, and listen to what I say. Indeed, these are not drunk, as you suppose, for it is only nine o'clock in the morning." (Vv. 14–15)

"You that are Israelites, listen to what I have to say: Jesus of Nazareth, a man attested to you by God with deeds of power, wonders, and signs that God did through him among you, as you yourselves know—this man, handed over to you according to the definite plan and foreknowledge of God, you crucified and killed by the hands of those outside the law. But God raised him up, having freed him from death, because it was impossible for him to be held in its power." (Vv. 22–24)

Peter said to them, "Repent, and be baptized every one of you in the name of Jesus Christ so that your sins may be forgiven; and you will receive the gift of the Holy Spirit. For the promise is for you, for your children, and for all who are far away, everyone whom the Lord our God calls to him." . . . So those who welcomed his message were baptized, and that day about three thousand persons were added. (Vv. 38–41)

Questions on the Scripture Passage

- What does Peter tell the Israelites about Jesus?
- What does Peter tell them they need to do?
- Three thousand are baptized after this discourse. What experience helped you own your faith?

Personal Questions

- Would you have believed in Jesus if you had lived when Jesus did?
- What transformations are being asked of us?
- What do you think the church will look like in ten years?

Petitions

For all those who newly embrace faith in Jesus Christ, we pray . . .

For those who help transform the church into the Body of Christ, the people of God, we pray . . .

(Add your own intentions.)

Concluding Prayer

Jesus, you left this earth so that the Spirit would come upon your church and upon us. Help us to be witnesses by word and example of the spirit of God working in our lives. Help us to be the molders of the future church. Amen.

Additional resource. *Parishes That Excel: Models of Excellence in Education, Ministry, and Evangelization,* by Patrick J. Brennan (Crossroad Publishing Co.).

God of Surprises

Jesus in his ministry teaches us about God's surprising ways. We want to think that God's ways are our ways, but they are not. We plan and plot, organize and seek control. Then something unexpected and unplanned happens. For example, we break a foot, a hip, or a hand. Our life changes. Suddenly, what was so important yesterday takes second place so that we can accomplish what is needed, such as being patient to allow healing. Life and the surprises of God teach us many of the lessons we need to learn as human beings.

Reading: The Woman with a Hemorrhage (Luke 8:43–48)

As he went, the crowds pressed in on him. Now there was a woman who had been suffering from hemorrhages for twelve years; and though she had spent all she had on physicians, no one could cure her. She came up behind him and touched the fringe of his clothes, and immediately her hemorrhage stopped. Then Jesus asked, "Who touched me?" When all denied it, Peter said, "Master, the crowds surround you and press in on you." But Jesus said, "Someone touched me; for I noticed that power had gone out from me." When the woman saw that she could not remain hidden, she came trembling; and falling down before him, she declared in the presence of all the people why she had touched him, and how she had been immediately healed. He said to her, "Daughter, your faith has made you well; go in peace."

Questions on the Scripture Passage

- Why, do you think, is the woman surprised that she is healed by touching Jesus' garment?
- Why, do you think, is Jesus surprised that power has gone from him?
- Jesus tells the woman that her faith has saved her, and then sends her off with words of peace. What does this mean to you?

Personal Questions

- How do you typically react to surprises? Can you think of particular examples?
- Would life be better without surprises, without risks?
- How does God speak to you in the surprises of life?

Petitions

That we will be open to the surprises God gives to us, we pray . . .

That we will recognize the moments of mystery, awe, and surprise we experience, we pray . . .

(Add your own intentions.)

Concluding Prayer

God of surprises, you place before us many unexpected obstacles and opportunities. They send us in new directions and often change our lives. Help us, God, to be open to all you reveal to us as we take risks and respond to what life asks of us. Amen.

Additional resource. *Invisible Lines of Connection: Sacred Stories of the Ordinary,* by Lawrence Kushner (Jewish Lights Publishing).

Understanding the Mass

Sometimes the things we do become so routine that we forget the reasons why we do them. A good example is going to Mass, where we gather as a parish community to hear the word of God and to break bread together in order to nourish ourselves for our faith journey. We get together as a community to give one another support, encouragement, and hope. We listen, celebrate, and share life-giving food so that when we are sent out we can "go in peace to love and serve the Lord."

Reading: A Discourse on the Bread of Life (John 6:29–58, NAB)

Jesus . . . said to them, "This is the work of God, that you believe in the one he sent." So they said to him, "What sign can you do, that we may see and believe in you? What can you do? Our ancestors ate manna in the desert, as it is written:

'He gave them bread from heaven to eat.'"

So Jesus said to them, "Amen, amen, I say to you, it was not Moses who gave the bread from heaven; my Father gives you the true bread from heaven. For the bread of God is that which comes down from heaven and gives life to the world."

So they said to him, "Sir, give us this bread always." Jesus said to them, "I am the bread of life; whoever comes to me will never hunger, and whoever believes in me will never thirst. But I told you that although you have seen [me], you do not believe. Everything that the Father gives me will come to me, and I will not reject anyone who comes to me, because I came down from heaven not to do my own will but the will of the one who sent me. And this is the will of the one who sent me, that I should not lose anything of what he gave me, but that I should raise it [on] the last day. For this is the will of my Father, that everyone who sees the Son and believes in him may have eternal life, and I shall raise him [on] the last day."

Questions on the Scripture Passage

- When Jesus says, "I am the bread of life," what is he telling us?
- What does Jesus ask of us?
- What is the promise of eternal life, and how do we receive it? Does it influence how we live?

Personal Questions

- What meaning does going to Mass hold for you? Has that meaning changed in your lifetime?
- What does receiving the body and blood of Christ mean to you?
- Do you see yourself as the bread of life for others because you participate at Mass?

Petitions

That God will bless those who take Communion to our homebound sisters and brothers, we pray . . .

That parishes will come together at Mass as supporting, encouraging, and sharing communities, we pray . . .

(Add your own intentions.)

Concluding Prayer

Bread of Life, thank you for the gift of the Eucharist, which gives us the opportunity to support, encourage, and share our lives with one another. May we become the bread of life for one another. Amen.

Additional resource. *How to Understand the Liturgy,* by Jean Lebon (Crossroad Publishing Co.).

Seashore Days

Peace can often be found while walking barefoot in the sand and the sea. The waves roll in and out. Tides turn. Sun dances across the water, against the whitecaps crashing along the shoreline. Mist sprays your face as the wind catches the waves. The seashore stands as the boundary between the surety of the solid ground and the mystery of the rolling sea.

Reading: Jesus by the Seashore (John 21:1–14)

After these things Jesus showed himself again to the disciples by the Sea of Tiberias; and he showed himself in this way. Gathered there together were Simon Peter, Thomas called the Twin, Nathanael of Cana in Galilee, the sons of Zebedee, and two others of his disciples. Simon Peter said to them, "I am going fishing." They said to him, "We will go with you." They went out and got into the boat, but that night they caught nothing.

Just after daybreak, Jesus stood on the beach; but the disciples did not know that it was Jesus. Jesus said to them, "Children, you have no fish, have you?" They answered him, "No." He said to them, "Cast the net to the right side of the boat, and you will find some." So they cast it, and now they were not able to haul it in because there were so many fish. That disciple whom Jesus loved said to Peter, "It is the Lord!" When Simon Peter heard that it was the Lord, he put on some clothes, for he was naked, and jumped into the sea. But the other disciples came in the boat, dragging the net full of fish, for they were not far from the land, only about a hundred yards off.

When they had gone ashore, they saw a charcoal fire there, with fish on it, and bread. Jesus said to them, "Bring some of the fish that you have just caught." So Simon Peter went aboard and hauled the net ashore, full of large fish, a hundred fifty-three of them; and though there were so many, the net was not torn. Jesus said to them, "Come and have breakfast." Now none of the disciples dared to ask him, "Who are you?" because they knew it was the Lord. Jesus came and took the bread and gave it to them, and did the same with the fish. This was now the third time that Jesus appeared to the disciples after he was raised from the dead.

Questions on the Scripture Passage

- Why, do you think, are the appearance stories about the risen Jesus in the Bible?
- What would it be like to eat with Jesus by the seashore as the disciples did?
- Why, do you think, do the disciples need to see Jesus after the Resurrection?

Personal Questions

- If you had lived in Jesus' time, what would this fishing story have meant to you?
- Would you have believed that was Jesus on the shoreline? Why or why not?
- The seashore is a wonderful mixture of mystery and reality. Some people believe that it is a good place to meet Jesus, who is real and yet way beyond our comprehension. Do you agree?

Petitions

For those who make their living by fishing in the sea, we pray . . .

In gratitude for the times we felt close to God in nature, we pray . . .

(Add your own intentions.)

Concluding Prayer

O God, in the moments when we are close to the sea or water, renew and refresh our life. Help us to remember our Baptism, the Baptisms of our children, and what it means to feel the wonder of water. Help us to remember the moments we have walked by the seashore with you. Amen.

Additional resource. *Gift from the Sea,* by Anne Morrow Lindbergh (Random House).

Loneliness

At times we have a sense that we are all alone in the world and no one really cares about us. Though loneliness transcends age, it may be particularly tough in later years if we have lost some mobility and when friends and family have died or moved away. We may grow depressed, and sunless days of winter may make us feel lonely. But loneliness can be an opportunity as well as a trial. The pain of loneliness can urge us to reach out to other people, to seek new interests, and to pray to our ever present, loving God.

Reading: The Agony in the Garden (Mark 14:32–42)

They went to a place called Gethsemane; and [Jesus] said to his disciples, "Sit here while I pray." He took with him Peter and James and John, and began to be distressed and agitated. And he said to them, "I am deeply grieved, even to death; remain here, and keep awake." And going a little farther, he threw himself on the ground and prayed that, if it were possible, the hour might pass from him. He said, "Abba, Father, for you all things are possible; remove this cup from me; yet, not what I want, but what you want." He came and found them sleeping; and he said to Peter, "Simon, are you asleep? Could you not keep awake one hour? Keep awake and pray that you may not come into the time of trial; the spirit indeed is willing, but the flesh is weak." And again he went away and prayed, saying the same words. And once more he came and found them sleeping, for their eyes were very heavy; and they did not know what to say to him. He came a third time and said to them, "Are you still sleeping and taking your rest? Enough! The hour has come; the Son of Man is betrayed into the hands of sinners. Get up, let us be going. See, my betrayer is at hand."

Questions on the Scripture Passage

- Do you think Jesus would feel better if the disciples stayed awake? Why or why not?
- How does Jesus change as he prays and talks with God?
- Does this scene from Jesus' story help you feel closer to him?

Personal Questions

- What does loneliness feel like for you?
- What do you do for yourself when you are feeling lonely?
- What do you do for others when you see they are feeling lonely?
- Do you feel God's presence when you are lonely?

Petitions

That we may learn to meet loneliness as a call to reach out to others, we pray . . .

For those who reach out and help others who experience depression and loneliness, we pray . . .

(Add your own intentions.)

Concluding Prayer

Loving God, help us to reach out to those feeling depressed and alone. Help us to recall what it is like when we feel this way. We know from our human experience that reaching out to others helps loneliness. Give us the courage to do this. Amen.

Additional resource. *Chicken Soup for the Soul: 101 Stories to Open the Heart and Rekindle the Spirit,* compiled by Jack Canfield and Mark Victor Hansen (Health Communications).

The Body of Christ Active Today

As the Body of Christ in the world today, we are to help build the Reign of God. Our suffering, our service, our random acts of kindness, our weakness and fear, all should serve the Reign of God. We may not be rich or famous, but every ray of light that we shed, every word of thoughtful gratitude, every act of competent help helps.

Reading: The Mustard Seed (Matthew 13:31–35)

[Jesus] put before them another parable: "The kingdom of heaven is like a mustard seed that someone took and sowed in his field; it is the smallest of all the seeds, but when it has grown it is the greatest of shrubs and becomes a tree, so that the birds of the air come and make nests in its branches."

He told them another parable: "The kingdom of heaven is like yeast that a woman took and mixed in with three measures of flour until all of it was leavened."

Jesus told the crowds all these things in parables; without a parable he told them nothing. This was to fulfill what had been spoken through the prophet:

> "I will open my mouth to speak in parables;
> I will proclaim what has been hidden from the foundation of the world."

Questions on the Scripture Passage

- What do you understand by the mustard seed story?
- What does the bread story tell you about God's Reign?
- Why are these "hidden" truths?

Personal Questions

- Have you ever planted seeds in another's heart or mind and watched the outcome? Think of specific instances.
- What is it like to make bread, cookies, or anything from scratch?
- Can you share a story of a time you did something good for someone who did not know it was you?

Petitions

For the goodness we have done for other people, we pray . . .

For the times people have helped us, we pray . . .

(Add your own intentions.)

Concluding Prayer

Thank you, God, for the times we have reached out to others. Thank you for the generous spirit you have put within us. And thank you for the times others have helped us. Forgive us for the times we did not say thanks to them or to you. Amen.

Additional resource. *To Act Justly, Love Tenderly, Walk Humbly: An Agenda for Ministers,* by Walter Brueggemann et al. (Paulist Press).

The Good Shepherd

The Good Shepherd is a consoling image. Jesus is one who walks with us, guides us along the way, and offers the soothing sound of the shepherd's voice. Jesus has a great concern and love for us. Should we lose our way, Jesus will leave the ninety-nine to come find us. Our Good Shepherd is always with us.

Reading: The Good Shepherd (John 10:2–18)

"The one who enters by the gate is the shepherd of the sheep. The gatekeeper opens the gate for him, and the sheep hear his voice. He calls his own sheep by name and leads them out. When he has brought out all his own, he goes ahead of them, and the sheep follow him because they know his voice. They will not follow a stranger, but they will run from him because they do not know the voice of strangers." Jesus used this figure of speech with them, but they did not understand what he was saying to them.

So again Jesus said to them, "Very truly, I tell you, I am the gate for the sheep. All who came before me are thieves and bandits; but the sheep did not listen to them. I am the gate. Whoever enters by me will be saved, and will come in and go out and find pasture. The thief comes only to steal and kill and destroy. I came that they may have life, and have it abundantly.

"I am the good shepherd. The good shepherd lays down his life for the sheep. The hired hand, who is not the shepherd and does not own the sheep, sees the wolf coming and leaves the sheep and runs away—and the wolf snatches them and scatters them. The hired hand runs away because a hired hand does not care for the sheep. I am the good shepherd. I know my own and my own know me, just as the Father knows me and I know the Father. And I lay down my life for the sheep. I have other sheep that do not belong to this fold. I must bring them also, and they will listen to my voice. So there will be one flock, one shepherd. For this reason the Father loves me, because I lay down my life in order to take it up again. No one takes it from me, but I lay it down of my own accord. I have power to lay it down, and I have power to take it up again. I have received this command from my Father."

Questions on the Scripture Passage

- In the Good Shepherd story, do you find the picture of Jesus consoling? Why or why not?
- How does Jesus care for the lost?
- What is Jesus freely willing to do for us?

Personal Questions

- Have you ever been consoled by Jesus?
- Has Jesus made you feel safe at times? If so, how?
- When have you done something freely with no strings attached?

Petitions

For those who reach out to console others, we pray . . .

For those who reach out to someone who has made a mistake, we pray . . .

(Add your own intentions.)

CONCLUDING PRAYER

Good Shepherd, guide us as we help a child, an adult son or daughter, a friend who has lost faith, or someone who has been unkind to us. At times, all of us need someone to show us the way. Be our shepherd and give us courage and strength on our way. Amen.

ADDITIONAL RESOURCE. *Small Miracles: Extraordinary Coincidences from Everyday Life,* by Vitta Halberstam and Judith Leventhal (Adams Media Corp.).

The Loss of Our Spouse

One of the greatest losses in life must be that of a spouse with whom we have shared a lifetime. We may be surprised by the range of feelings we experience. The sense of physical loss—of simply not seeing our loved one again in human form—or the sense of grief in not being able to touch that person again may be with us for a long time. Feelings of guilt or anger may overwhelm us. What would we have done, if only we had known he or she was going to die? We can grieve and eventually let go, but we are changed.

Reading: The Burial (John 19:38–42)

After these things, Joseph of Arimathea, who was a disciple of Jesus, though a secret one because of his fear of the Jews, asked Pilate to let him take away the body of Jesus. Pilate gave him permission; so he came and removed his body. Nicodemus, who had at first come to Jesus by night, also came, bringing a mixture of myrrh and aloes, weighing about a hundred pounds. They took the body of Jesus and wrapped it with the spices in linen cloths, according to the burial custom of the Jews. Now there was a garden in the place where he was crucified, and in the garden there was a new tomb in which no one had ever been laid. And so, because it was the Jewish day of Preparation, and the tomb was nearby, they laid Jesus there.

Questions on the Scripture Passage

- What gives Joseph of Arimathea the courage to ask for the body of Jesus?
- What is the Jewish day of Preparation?
- Why are the rituals to Jesus' body so important for Nicodemus?

Personal Questions

- What are your family's rituals for funerals?
- How do family and friends help at the time of a death?
- How can we put our life back together after the death of a loved one, especially our spouse?
- Does belief in eternal life help in our grief?

Petitions

For those who have lost a spouse in death, that we may remember them, we pray . . .

That the pain and grief of losing a spouse may find healing in our belief in the Resurrection, we pray . . .

(Add your own intentions.)

Concluding Prayer

God of healing, we know that death is a part of our human condition. Jesus shared our humanity, so shared our death. Be with us as we walk this journey of suffering, and bring us to the fullness of life through the Resurrection. We ask this prayer in your name. Amen.

Additional resource. *Cries of the Heart: Praying Our Losses,* by Wayne Simsic (Saint Mary's Press).

Traveling

If you have ever had the opportunity to travel, you know how wonderful it can be to experience the beauty of the ocean, the desert, the landmarks of Boston, New York, the Grand Canyon, or the Rocky Mountains. Paris, Rome, Kyoto, and Sydney all have their allurements. However, distance and strangeness are not so important. We can "travel" even in our hometown. What is important is that we try to see fully, enjoy, and appreciate the newness of each day and each place. Traveling is more a state of opening our mind and our senses than it is a matter of crossing oceans and continents. Seniors can be great travelers when they learn to relax, visit old friends, make new ones, and enjoy the beauty of the world around them.

Reading: Apostolic Traveling (Luke 10:1–9)

After this the Lord appointed seventy others and sent them on ahead of him in pairs to every town and place where he himself intended to go. He said to them, "The harvest is plentiful, but the laborers are few; therefore ask the Lord of the harvest to send out laborers into his harvest. Go on your way. See, I am sending you out like lambs into the midst of wolves. Carry no purse, no bag, no sandals; and greet no one on the road. Whatever house you enter, first say, 'Peace to this house!' And if anyone is there who shares in peace, your peace will rest on that person; but if not, it will return to you.

Remain in the same house, eating and drinking whatever they provide, for the laborer deserves to be paid. Do not move about from house to house. Whenever you enter a town and its people welcome you, eat what is set before you; cure the sick who are there, and say to them, 'The kingdom of God has come near to you.'"

Questions on the Scripture Passage

- According to Jesus, how should Christians greet people while traveling?
- What does it mean when Jesus tells the disciples to say, "The kingdom of God has come near to you"?
- Why is traveling light a good idea today, just as it was when Jesus spoke?

Personal Questions

- What is your favorite place to visit? Why?
- Can you share some meaningful things that have happened to you in your travels?
- Where was God most present to you in your travels?

Petitions

For a greater appreciation of the world that God has created, we pray . . .

For the people, cultures, and countries we have visited, we pray . . .

(Add your own intentions.)

Concluding Prayer

We are grateful for the gift of our world and all the beauty that is around us, God. Thank you for the places we have had a chance to visit. Help us always to appreciate the many people we have met along the way. May our sharing together change the world and make it a better place. Amen.

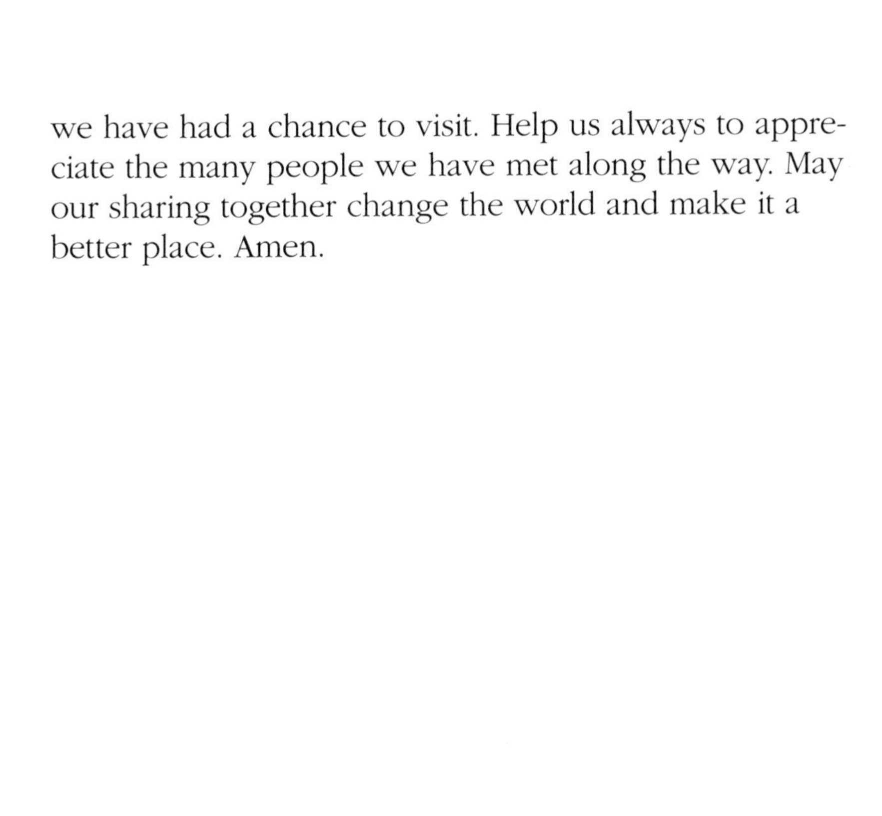

ADDITIONAL RESOURCES. Any travel book or magazine, such as *National Geographic*.

A video on travel available from the library or video store.

Building the Reign of God

Jesus is our example of how we are to live and how we are to build the Reign of God. We are the hands and feet that continue the work of Jesus. The spirit of God touches our lives, helping us to feed those who are hungry, to clothe those who are naked, to visit those who are sick, to uplift those who are poor, and to heal those who are brokenhearted. We help bring the dream of God into reality by working for the Reign of God.

Reading: For I Was Hungry (Matthew 25:35–40)

[On the throne of glory, the Son of God will say,] "For I was hungry and you gave me food, I was thirsty and you gave me something to drink, I was a stranger and you welcomed me, I was naked and you gave me clothing, I was sick and you took care of me, I was in prison and you visited me." Then the righteous will answer him, "Lord, when was it that we saw you hungry and gave you food, or thirsty and gave you something to drink? And when was it that we saw you a stranger and welcomed you, or naked and gave you clothing? And when was it that we saw you sick or in prison and visited you?" And the king will answer them, "Truly I tell you, just as you did it to one of the least of these who are members of my family, you did it to me."

Questions on the Scripture Passage

- In this passage who are the righteous?
- How simple or difficult are the how-tos in this passage?
- What do we mean when we say, "What we do for one another, we do for Jesus"?

Personal Questions

- How has helping others changed your life?
- How have you shown mercy?
- How have you reached out in the civic community or your neighborhood to help others?

Petitions

That we may reach out to help those in need, we pray . . .

That we may remember to thank those who show us simple kindnesses, we pray . . .

(Add your own intentions.)

Concluding Prayer

God of welcoming, by your example you have taught us how to love, forgive, and heal. Give us a generous spirit to continue your work for your coming Reign. Amen.

Additional resource. *Mirror Meditations: Praying with the Images of Vatican II,* by Robert L. Kinast (Liturgical Press).

Volunteering

Many retired people want to use their skills and years of experience, so they volunteer at a soup kitchen, hospital, social-service agency, church, school, library, Red Cross agency, or nursing home. Volunteers are of tremendous value to the civic and church communities, giving untold hours of service each year. Communities are blessed with the many people who contribute their time and talents. Volunteering is a two-way street too. Those who volunteer keep learning, growing, and expanding their capacity for love.

Reading: Jesus Feeds Five Thousand (Matthew 14:13–20)

Now when Jesus heard this, he withdrew from there in a boat to a deserted place by himself. But when the crowds heard it, they followed him on foot from the towns. When he went ashore, he saw a great crowd; and he had compassion for them and cured their sick. When it was evening, the disciples came to him and said, "This is a deserted place, and the hour is now late; send the crowds away so that they may go into the villages and buy food for themselves." Jesus said to them, "They need not go away; you give them something to eat." They replied, "We have nothing here but five loaves and two fish." And he said, "Bring them here to me." Then he ordered the crowds to sit down on the grass. Taking the five loaves and the two fish, he looked up to heaven, and blessed and broke the loaves, and gave them to the disciples, and the disciples gave them to the crowds. And all ate and were filled; and they took up what was left over of the broken pieces, twelve baskets full.

Questions on the Scripture Passage

- Why is Jesus' heart so moved by the crowd?
- Why, do you think, is it important for everyone to sit down?
- What food do the disciples have in the beginning, and what is left after everyone eats? What happens with the food?

Personal Questions

- What opportunities for volunteer work exist in your community?
- What does volunteering mean to you?
- What return do you receive for volunteering?

Petitions

For all the many agencies and churches that need the help of volunteers, we pray . . .

For the retired people who give of their time to help others, we pray . . .

(Add your own intentions.)

Concluding Prayer

Compassionate God, you have blessed many retired people with the desire to help others. Give them health and all they need in order to reach out to others with their blessings. Amen.

Suggested action. Visit civic, service, or church agencies that are open to receiving volunteers.

Resurrection

We know that Jesus rose from the dead, and our faith tells us that we, too, will rise from the dead. As we mature in age, we realize that one day we will die. The promise of our own resurrection brings us face-to-face with what that reality means.

Reading: Jesus Appears to the Eleven (Luke 24:36–49)

While they were talking about this, Jesus himself stood among them and said to them, "Peace be with you." They were startled and terrified, and thought that they were seeing a ghost. He said to them, "Why are you frightened, and why do doubts arise in your hearts? Look at my hands and my feet; see that it is I myself. Touch me and see; for a ghost does not have flesh and bones as you see that I have." And when he had said this, he showed them his hands and his feet. While in their joy they were disbelieving and still wondering, he said to them. "Have you anything here to eat?" They gave him a piece of broiled fish, and he took it and ate in their presence.

Then he said to them, "These are my words that I spoke to you while I was still with you—that everything written about me in the law of Moses, the prophets, and the psalms must be fulfilled." Then he opened their minds to understand the scriptures, and he said to them, "Thus it is written, that the Messiah is to suffer and to rise from the dead on the third day, and that repentance and forgiveness of sins is to be proclaimed in his name to all nations, beginning from Jerusalem. You are witnesses of these things. And see, I am sending upon you what my Father promised; so stay here in the city until you have been clothed with power from on high."

Questions on the Scripture Passage

- What is Jesus' greeting? How does he want the Apostles to feel?
- What does Luke say about the Messiah?
- What does Jesus ask the Apostles to do concerning the Spirit?

Personal Questions

- When have you faced your own death?
- How has your faith matured in your belief about the Resurrection?
- What does the Resurrection mean to you?

Petitions

For the times we have failed to recognize Christ in one another, we pray . . .

That we may strive to see the best in one another, we pray . . .

(Add your own intentions.)

Concluding Prayer

Risen Christ, we know that you are in our midst when we gather together. We have moments when you reveal yourself to us more fully and help us to see. Help us to recognize you in one another, and forgive us when we do not. Amen.

Additional resource. *Good Goats: Healing Our Image of God,* by Dennis Linn (Paulist Press).